ARIZONA GHOST STORIES

ANTONIO R. GARCEZ

RED RABBIT PRESS
SILVER CITY, NEW MEXICO

Other titles by Antonio R. Garcez:
New Mexico Ghost Stories ISBN 0-9634029-9-4
American Indian Ghost Stories of the Southwest ISBN 0-9634029-7-8
Ghost Stories of California's Gold Rush Country &
Yosemite National Park   ISBN 0-9634029-8-6

1st edition—1995
2nd edition—2003
3rd edition—2005

ISBN Number 0-9740988-0-9

*The author may be contacted for public appearances
at the following address:*
Antonio R. Garcez • Red Rabbit Press
4129 N. Gold St.
Silver City, NM 88061

Some of the places that appear in these stories have changed
ownership or names since the first printing of this book.
Some of the individuals whose stories appear in this book have,
since its first printing, moved on, either in this world, or to the next.
Their stories appear here as they were directly related to the author
at the time they were interviewed.

Cover & book design and typography by
Kathleen Sparkes, White Hart Design
Editing by Kate Willis

Praises for
ARIZONA GHOST STORIES
by Antonio R. Garcez

"ARIZONA GHOST STORIES gives a hauntingly accurate overview to the many reports of haunted sites all over the state. It not only lists the places from north to south but quotes the interviews of eyewitnesses giving a remarkable feeling of being there with them as they encounter the unknown. Such sites as the Copper Queen Hotel in Bisbee to the Jerome Inn come to life in Mr. Garcez's investigations. His chapter on the reports of ghosts at Tombstone is perhaps one of the best accounts I have seen on this subject."

—Richard Senate

"The accounts range from sweetly sentimental to truly terrifying, but all share the benefit of Antonio's sensitivity and attention to detail. He shows respect for the tales, and those who tell them, and understands that history and culture are inextricably bound to all folklore."

—Jo-Anne Christensen

"Arizona could not have asked for a better chronicler of its supernatural landscape than Antonio R. Garcez. From Arivaca to Yuma, Arizona's most haunted places are all here! These stories will send shivers up your spine, and rightly so—they all really took place! If you ever wanted to experience something paranormal, let this book be your guide!"

—Dennis William Hauck

"These are not long-ago cowboy yarns, but very real, very current ghost stories from a rich and chilling mix of voices. Antonio has a rare talent for telling detail; he paints unforgettably creepy images that linger long after the book is done."

—Chris Woodyard

"The reader is transported into the world of the supernatural, by a great storyteller who weaves history and personal interviews into a series of riveting tales, sure to make your skin crawl! Here, restless spirits of the past meet present-day skeptics head on. Memories come to life in the stories from 19 diverse Arizona counties. The thoughtfully told, well-researched stories are sometimes frightening, oftentimes chilling, and always fascinating."

—Rob & Anne Wlodarski

Praises for
NEW MEXICO GHOST STORIES
by Antonio R. Garcez

"This collection of personal encounters with the 'spiritual' or 'supernatural' certainly supported some of my own experiences. These stories are made more frightening by their very proximity."
—*Stephanie Gonzales, NM Secretary of State*

"I highly recommend that both local citizens and visitors to Santa Fe read this book!"   —*Sam Pick, Mayor-Santa Fe, NM*

"Fascinating to read ... offers the reader insight into our town's unique traditions, folklore and history; don't miss it!"
—*Frederick A. Peralta, Mayor-Town of Taos*

"Important documentation of the people and history of northern New Mexico. Keep writing!"
—*Kathleen Knoth, Librarian, Millicent Rogers Museum, Taos NM*

"At last someone has written a book about the ghost tales people have been telling here for years!"
—*Tom Sharpe, Albuquerque Journal*

"It's enough to send shivers right up your spine! An excellent effort by Antonio Garcez and I anxiously await his next book!"
—*Dale Kaczmarek, Ghost Research Society*

"If you're a lover of the supernatural, get cozy in an easy chair and prepare your self for the inevitable. Eyewitness accounts told in a straightforward manner!"
—*Tim Palmieri, Western Outlaw-Lawman History Association*

"Another terrifying book from Garcez ... ! "
—*Chris Woodyard, Invisible Ink-Books on Ghosts Hauntings*

"Highly Entertaining!"
—*Mary A. Sarber, Texas Book Columnist, El Paso, Herald-Post*

Contents

Foreword

I discovered the work of Antonio R. Garcez while vacationing in Santa Fe. We were going to be there for the better part of a week, and although I'd brought along several books to read at night in our hotel, none of them really interested me, and I spent that first evening watching television. The next morning, in the hotel's gift shop, I came across a volume titled, *American Indian Ghost Stories of the Southwest*. The cover featured what appeared to be an Apache skeleton riding a horse through the desert night, with lightning flashing across the sky above two, tall, silhouetted saguaros.

I bought it immediately.

I started reading the book that afternoon. After a busy morning sightseeing, window shopping, and taking an historic walking tour, we ate lunch at one of Santa Fe's many renowned restaurants and then returned to the hotel for a brief rest before heading up Canyon Road to visit art galleries. My three-year-old son was on the bed in the room, taking a nap, and my wife was next to me on the balcony outside of our suite, thumbing through one of the tourist magazines the hotel had provided. It was a warm day, and from down below I could hear the sounds of traffic and brief snatches of conversation from other visitors walking by. It was not an atmosphere conducive to fright, yet as I sat there in the sun, I had chills.

I was reading the story of Sofita Becera, in a chapter titled "Historic Santa Fe," the tale of a woman haunted by a spirit attached to a stolen *molcajete* (a stone mortar used by Native Americans to grind herbs and spices), and the incidents that occurred to her closely paralleled fictional events from my recently published novel, *The Return*.

Only, what happened to Sofita Becera was much creepier than anything in my book.

I sped through the rest of *American Indian Ghost Stories*

of the Southwest, thrilled by the unique tales within the volume. I was impressed with Garcez's clear, straightforward writing style and his ability to draw out from people their personal supernatural experiences—so impressed, that I wrote him a fan letter immediately upon returning home to California. We've been corresponding ever since, and I have since read *Adobe Angels: The Ghosts of Santa Fe and Taos,* his excellent compilation of north-central New Mexico ghost stories, and have been eagerly looking forward to reading his other books.

So when Antonio sent me a copy of *Ghost Stories of Arizona* and asked if I would like to write an introduction to the new edition of the book, I jumped at the chance.

If anything, the stories in this book are even scarier than those in Antonio's New Mexico books. Maybe I'm prejudiced, because I'm from Arizona and am thus more familiar with the locations of these hauntings, but to my mind, these narratives are more intrinsically frightening than those of his previous collections—the ghostly encounters are creepier, more threatening. While reading several of the accounts, I found myself experiencing that delicious frisson that comes from a truly terrifying tale.

And I'm not a person who's easily spooked.

The most exciting thing about this volume, however, is that when I read it for the first time, nearly all of the stories were new to me. These aren't the recycled myths of my childhood; those urban, suburban, and rural legends appropriated by Arizonans and transplanted to their state, like the Big Foot knockoff, The Mogollon Monster, or La Llorona, a New Mexican ghost (who, in the bastardized version I heard, haunted the open canals of Phoenix in the 1960s). No, the tales here are quirkier, more intimate, more obscure, and what grants them the stamp of authenticity, what makes them not only believable but truly chilling, is the fact that they're not typical, traditional ghost stories with pat explanations and simplistic cause-and-effect plot lines. Nearly all of these hauntings are open-ended, the cause and origins of the sightings are not neatly spelled out, and the occurrences are not tied up with easy resolutions. Rather, they're random incidents, resonating with the vague, inexplicable logic of the unknown. There are a few famous hauntings—the Cooper Queen Hotel in Bisbee, two buildings in Jerome—but for the most part, the focus is on unfamiliar episodes in out-of-the-way locations, and that's what gives this book its singular power.

While the work of Antonio R. Garcez is extremely interesting and entertaining, particularly to those of us who enjoy a good scare, I also believe it performs an important historical/sociological function: setting down the unwritten history of an overlooked subject—paranormal experiences in the Southwest. Although he's a terrific writer, I think it's Antonio's skills as an interviewer and oral historian that set his work apart from other chroniclers of the paranormal, many of whom seem to rely on thirdhand recitations of events, rather than going straight to the source. Antonio gets his information directly from the horse's mouth, and allows the participants to tell their own stories in their own ways. He also does his homework, and in a few brief introductory paragraphs always manages to give a historical perspective and context to these individual experiences. In the case of this book, he illuminates many previously unknown incidents of ghostly phenomenas, preserving for posterity accounts that would otherwise remain untold.

I won't waste any more of your time singing the praises of *Ghost Stories of Arizona*. It's in your hands, and you're about to turn the page and jump headlong into these tales of otherworldly encounters by everyday people. Suffice it to say that you are in for a treat, and whether or not you believe in the supernatural, I suggest you set aside a large enough block of time to read the entire book, because you're not going to be able to put it down.

Oh, and make sure you leave the light on.

—*Bentley Little*

Preface

"There was no climate or soil . . . equal to that of Arizona . . . It is my land, my home, my father's land . . . I want to spend my last days there, and to be buried among those mountains."
—*Geronimo*

Though I live in the neighboring state of New Mexico, Arizona has always remained for me a source of wonder. The name Arizona has a unique magic, which few other states of the union can conger. Arizona is a state of mind. A state born of ancient cliff dwellers, and modern-day native people endowed by their particular cultural legacies of art, technology, science, herbology, hydrology, etc. Arizona is also a state of historical character, a character wrought by individuals of grand personal dreams, of marginal economic means, of extraordinary immigrations, and of stubborn tenacity. Indeed Arizona is composed of many Arizonas.

In this book I've attempted to draw from Arizona's vast human resource, and to present for the first time a collection of its particular ghost stories. This book has a twofold purpose: first, to offer the first ever book of Arizona ghost stories; second, to introduce open minds to the possibility that, with a bit of investigation and reflection, ghosts do exist.

It is not my intention to have the answer, to prove why ghosts exist; why they present themselves to only certain individuals and not others. The attempt to provide an explanation to this concept has been presented over and over again by numerous other writers, both sincere and insincere. The fact remains that the living cannot define ghosts, ghosts control their own definitions!

Ghosts, spirits, entities, souls, specters, apparitions, etc., have always played a recognized role in the family structure, the arts: poetry, song, dance of the American Indian and the Spanish-speaking. Are these two cultural groups more of a target for ghosts? Not likely. I believe that simply these groups, given their social and spiritual complexities, make them more sensitive to the possibility that ghosts do exist. The traditions of burial rites, symbology, and the belief in the duality of life and death, are very much a part of their ceremonial observances. But they are not entirely unique.

Even before recorded history, there was a universal experience of ghosts that established itself into culture, language, and folklore throughout the world. Accounts that have out lasted the test of time clearly state, that the living have genuinely seen and been in direct contact with ghosts or spirits. The vast majority of these experiences are positive. Ghosts can be independent of the living, but the living cannot be independent of ghosts.

Given the research and investigation I've gathered from all my books, I have come to recognize that making contact with a spirit or ghost is not all that difficult; conversely it is an extremely common phenomenon. Contact may not just be visual. It may also be associated with hearing, a "feeling", smell and touch.

Throughout history, one of the most insistent and deeply emotional human desires is to know what becomes of us when we die. So many unanswered questions, and possibilities remain.

Further, this book is a vehicle. A vehicle in which the reader's imagination is transported with the help of their own real experiences, fantasies, and dreams to a place of the powerful, the surreal and the unknown.

It would be impossible to gather a collection of ghost stories where each story is of equal worth. But as you will discover, each of the stories contained within these pages is original, and hopefully is presented as it was passionately described to me by the interviewee.

Keep in mind, these stories are but only a sampling of the wealth of other yet to be recorded stories that exist in Arizona. I will no doubt be working on a future second book, publishing these unrecorded experiences. However, I am confident that the stories contained within the pages of the book you are holding, will continue to convey for years to come, the test of repeated readings. Perhaps when all is said, my purpose was simply to create a sense of "connectiveness," a union between us and "Them."

Foremost, it is easy to overemphasize the negative aspects of a ghost as being evil, scary, etc. However, to focus on these simplistic points alone, constitutes neither a positive nor hopeful view of our own end result. The best definition of the existence of ghosts must be viewed through our own traditions. Therefore, I am inclined to believe that ghosts do exist and are manifest among us.

Lastly, I am well aware that since the release date of my first edition of this book, there have been other "writers" who have followed behind my lead, by transcribing their own "attempts" at ghost books. I am both profoundly amused by these nimble endeavors yet, remain disturbed by their lack of convincing, erudite authority.

Be that as it is, for the record, know that I am deeply touched at the debt of gratitude by which you the readers of my books have uninterruptedly bestowed upon me, via your numerous correspondences. I thank you and wish you all "protection from the night"... metaphorically speaking.

—*Antonio R. Garcez*

Acknowledgements

*I wish to thank the following individuals
for their support and assistance:*

Henry C. Estrada

Arizona Department of Commerce
Don Harris, Communications Director,
Mary Melendez, Administrative Secretary,
for the use of each cities Community Profile.

Arizona State Parks
History of Yuma Territorial Prison, Picture of John Ryan.

Jerome Chamber of Commerce/Jerome Historical Society
History of Clinkscale building.

Yuma Department of Community Redevelopment/
Yuma Convention and Visitors Bureau
History of Yuma County Courthouse.

Robert Altherr • *History of Jerome Grand Hotel.*

Holbrook Chamber of Commerce/
Historical Society of Navajo County
*Invitations to hanging of George Smiley and Deposition of
T. J. McSweeny Steve and Gloria Goldstein*
original documents held at Arizona State Archives,
Department of Library Archives and Public Records

Craig H. Rothen
The Legend of "The Swamper," Photo of "Howard."

Albuquerque Rattlesnake Museum, New Mexico.

And my own personal thanks to the men, women, and children
of Arizona with HIV/AIDS and their caregivers.
You are all our teachers and truly our living angels.

*...and especially to every person whom
I interviewed for this book.*

Dedication

To my brother Vincent R. Garcez,
I will always be grateful

And to my partner, Henry C. Estrada,
who dreams with me.

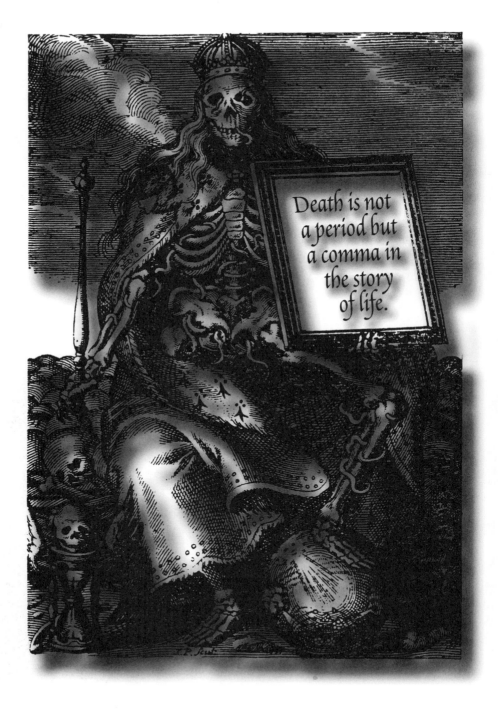

Death is not a period but a comma in the story of life.

Introduction

Before deciding to write a book about Arizona's ghost stories, I checked the usual sources to begin my research: libraries, bookstores, etc. I was genuinely surprised to discover that there were no books to be found on the subject. There were plenty of books on ghost towns and legends of the West, but there were no books devoted specifically to *ghosts*. Amazing.

Given its particular wealth of land, culture, people, and unique history, I felt that the state of Arizona was long overdue for a collection of ghost stories. The stories of gunfighters, lovers, ranchers, miners, convicts, business owners, farmers, and Native American points of view all are included in this book. Families, and friends we knew, spoke to, walked with, played with, who now lie under Arizona adobe soil are in this book. Men, women, and children who wait tirelessly for us in and among desert landscapes, houses, bars, hotels, and shaded avenues—they too are in this book. These memories, brought back to life, have come forth to re-enter our world of the living.

You'll find them all within these pages— the murmuring voices; darting shadows; misty faces twisted in silent screams; empty, staring eyes of the wronged; angry booted footsteps of the condemned; and the vaporous svelte bodies of women with dark, empty-eyed sockets. They are all here.

Ghosts offer the living not only curious, and sometimes terrifying, fodder for stories and folklore, but also insight into another world in which time and space cease to exist. These samples of stories from Arizona provide readers with engaging reading and a bit of a history lesson as well.

Now relax, find a comfortable chair, fix yourself a strong pot of campfire coffee and prepare yourself for a long and bumpy ride into the realm of Arizona's ghosts. Remember, it's best not to keep your hosts waiting long, although they do have all the time in the world, they anger much too easily. Reservations are not required, because after all, your arrival has been pre-confirmed—far in advance!

Enjoy!

ARIZONA
GHOST
STORIES

Arivaca

Arivaca, about 11 miles north of Arizona's border with Mexico, was mapped by Father Eusebio Kino in 1695. It is in an area that contains some of the oldest mines in the United States. Arivaca, which is unincorporated, is about 56 miles southwest of Tucson in southern Pima county.

The locale may have been a Tohono O'odham (Pima) Indian village before 1751, when natives revolted against the Spanish, who were attracted by precious metals and excellent grazing land. Mines developed by the Spaniards were worked by Native Americans under the direction of Tumacacori Mission padres. In 1833, the Mexican government approved a petition by brothers Tomas and Ignacio Ortiz to raise cattle and horses on 8,677 acres of land that formed the Aribac Ranch. "La Aribac" is an Native American word meaning "small springs." Although boundaries for the ranch were never certain, its rights were bought by the Sonora Exploring and Mining Company in 1856. This company operated mines near Arivaca and Tubac. Also located on the ranch were reduction works for the Heintzelman Mine. The post office was established in 1878.

Charles Poston, the father of Arizona, acquired the property in 1870 and later asked the U.S. government to confirm his right to 26,508 acres. The U.S. surveyor general recommended confirmation of 8,680 acres, but the U.S. Congress took no action. Poston's rights were obtained by the Arivaca Land and Cattle Company, which asked the U.S. Court of Private Land Claims to approve the land claim. The court refused, saying it was impossible to identify... the land which was intended to be granted. This decision was upheld by the U.S. Supreme Court on March 24, 1902, and the land became part of the public domain.

Arivaca now is primarily a retirement and residential area.

I interviewed Frances at her home in Arivaca, a small little town tucked within a quaint desert valley. Within this quiet town lies Frances's two-bedroom home. From the street, the house reveals no indication of what had transpired within its walls just a few years ago .

Frances preferred that I not describe the outside of her house; by doing so, some of her neighbors might know who she was and begin to gossip. Given her concern, I have chosen not to use her real name.

FRANCES TORRES'S STORY

My story about "El Coyote" took place just a couple of years ago. I have made sure not to tell many people about what happened in the house because, being a small town, the gossip gets around really quickly.

I used to rent and live in the house next to the one I live in now. I used to know the old woman who was the owner of the property. When I moved into the house next door, she and I began to talk, and we became very friendly with each other. Some mornings she and I would have coffee in my kitchen. She sure was a talker. She told me about her son, who lived in Tucson, and I got to meet him a few times before she died.

I recall that the first time I visited her, she showed me around the inside of her home. I noticed that one of her bedrooms had a door with nails hammered into the door frame. I asked her about this because it was very strange to have this door nailed shut the way it was. Hanging on one of the nails was a small metal crucifix. Her explanation was that she had nailed the door shut because of "El Coyote." I asked her, "Who was El Coyote?" She said he was a bad spirit that needed to be kept locked up. I thought to myself, "living by herself for so long has made this old woman go nuts." I asked her why the spirit had the name of El Coyote. She said she had given it that name because although she had never really seen the spirit's face, its body looked like a wild dog. By this time, I thought to myself that this poor woman needed to get out of the house more often and mingle with people.

I didn't think much more about the "friend" she kept locked up in the bedroom. I never heard any loud noises coming from her home, and after all, she was really sweet. One day, while she was at the post office, I walked to the rear of her house and looked inside the bedroom window where she kept El Coyote. I didn't know what I would expect to see.

Inside, I saw a room without any furniture. It didn't even have any rugs. "Poor old woman," I thought, " she must have invented this ghost as her own personal friend." I began to feel sorry for her because I myself have never married, and sometimes it does get lonely. But there wasn't anything unusual about the room, so I never mentioned it to her again.

Well, less than a year later, the woman spent Thanksgiving in Tucson with her son and his family. I know she was very happy because, after returning home, all she did was talk to me about how nice her visit had been.

Two days later, I paid her a visit to show her a large holiday greeting card that had arrived at my house. I knocked on her front door, and when she did not answer, I walked to the rear door, which was left unlocked, and walked inside. I immediately smelled gas. I took a few slow cautious steps into the house and kept calling her name. There was no answer. I got scared and quickly walked through the house. When I entered her bedroom, I found her lifeless body in bed. A flexible copper hose leading from the wall to her gas heater had developed a small hole.

After her funeral, her son told me that he was going to sell his mother's house. I asked him if he would sell it to me, and he agreed. I also asked him if he knew anything about the closed door that was nailed shut or about El Coyote. He said that his mother only mentioned El Coyote a few times but that he thought it was something crazy his mother had made up.

After I bought the house, two friends who lived in the town of Nogales came to Arivaca to help me with repairs. I was overjoyed to finally own a house of my own. I began to remove old wallpaper and paint every wall. Of course, the first thing I did was to remove the nails on the bedroom door where El Coyote lived. During the repair work, I never noticed any strange noise or saw any ghost. Finally after a few weeks, the house was ready for me to move in.

After moving all my belongings into the house, I soon began to notice that the rear bedroom was strangely very much colder than the rest of the house. At first I was not bothered by it, but then I began to wonder. Sometimes it was so cold that I got goose bumps on my arms. Other times, it was like stepping outside into a cool night. I thought about what the old woman had told me, but then I figured that my imagination was working overtime.

As the weeks passed, things began to get worse. Day and night I began to see strange shadows in the house. I don't mean shadows shaped like a person—they were more like a large blanket that covered the wall! One afternoon, I was washing dishes, and I heard a strange voice. Because I was in the kitchen, I had the volume on the TV in the living room turned up high, so that I could listen. I thought that perhaps the voice was coming from the television. I stopped washing the dishes because I felt a very strong feeling that someone was in the kitchen with me. I turned around to look behind me. I saw this huge black shadow—it covered the whole wall—move slowly, then quickly across the room and into the hallway.

It couldn't have been the shadow of a passing car because the kitchen is located in the rear of the house. A passing plane couldn't have caused it either, because it would have to be flying level with the house. No, I immediately knew this was something that had to do with the spiritual world. Even though I was a bit shaken, I walked into the hallway and looked in the bathroom, closet, and the bedrooms. As soon as I entered the last bedroom, immediately the cold feeling came over me. I knew I had to get out of there fast!

I closed the door behind me and left it closed until the following week, when I had someone pay me a visit. I had ordered a pair of new closet doors. They were delivered by a Nogales contractor who carried the new doors off his truck and into the bedroom. Everything was going fine. I was in the living room watching television while the sound of his electric drill was making a loud noise. I remember walking to the bedroom and asking the contractor if he wanted some coffee. He said "no," and I left him alone to finish the job of installing the doors.

Suddenly, I heard him yell, and as I began to rise off my chair, he came flying down the hallway and out the front door! I thought he had hurt himself, so I raced out the door to meet him at his truck, which was parked in the street. He was pale. He told me that "something" had taken hold of his arm. When he turned around he saw a very large man with angry eyes grabbing hold of his upper left arm. It took all the strength he had to free himself from the grip.

The contractor did not know anything about the bedroom or the woman who had owned the house before I did. His experience left him shaken. I myself was very concerned about spending any more nights or days in the house, with that "thing" walking about, but I volunteered to go back into the house and return with his tools. I softly prayed to myself as I walked into the bedroom, and I guess God helped me, because I did not see anything.

After the contractor had driven away, I walked back to the bedroom and placed a crucifix on the door and closed it. I decided to tell my cousin, who lives in the town just south of Arivaca, about what had happened. "If there is an angry spirit in the bedroom, it must be protecting something. Why wouldn't it want people in the bedroom?" she asked.

That weekend my cousin, her husband, Pablo, and a friend came to my house to investigate. We entered the bedroom and searched the closet and tapped on the walls. As we walked about the room, we all took turns walking over one particular spot on the floor that was colder than the rest of the room. "That's it, it's here!" my cousin said. "What ever this ghost is protecting, it's under this area of the floor."

Pablo went outside and located a small door that was an entrance to a crawl space under the house. He told us to get flashlights. The two men opened the door and entered the crawl space as my cousin and I watched. Soon we heard Pablo yell to us to come outside. The men had found something. As we all gathered in the yard, they showed us a small Indian pottery bowl and some old stone beads. No money, no bones—just a bowl and beads. We placed them into a cardboard box with crumbled up newspaper as packing material.

I didn't want these things in my house, I decided to take them to the nearby San Javier Del Bac mission at the Pima reservation. After driving up the mission driveway, I waited in my car for a moment, just to think things over. I wasn't sure if giving these Indian things to a priest would be the best thing to do. Instead I decided to take a short drive to the reservation office and talk to someone. I met an office worker and explained to her that I needed to know if there was a person who could help me. She gave me directions to the house of a woman who heals people on the reservation.

As I was parking the car on the dirt street, the woman and her son were driving up to the house. I introduced myself and quickly told her what I had in the cardboard box. She seemed uneasy, but said she would take care of it. My meeting with her only took

San Javier del Bac Mission

about 15 minutes. I know that I must have appeared very nervous, because I remember speaking to her very quickly. I took the cardboard box with the pot in it from my trunk and left it on her porch. As I drove away, I began to feel very comfortable and relaxed. I somehow knew that I had done the right thing. A feeling of relief came over me.

Since that night I have not had another experience with El Coyote in my house. Today, I use the bedroom as a workshop for the ceramic figurines I paint. In addition to figurines of people, I paint animals, and flowers, but if you look closely you'll notice I don't have one single painted pot. I guess you can tell why I stay away from keeping pots in that bedroom!

BISBEE

The town of Bisbee is located approximately 100 miles southeast of Tucson, directly in the heart of the Mule Mountains at 5,300 feet above sea level. The quaint town was founded in 1880, and thanks to its rich copper deposits, quickly developed to become the most populated settlement in the state. The town's mineral wealth did not go unnoticed by the Phelps Dodge mining company, who built a railroad into the town in 1880 and soon began to mine the rich ore. The many years of prosperity ended in the early 1970s when Phelps Dodge decided to cease operations. This in turn forced a good number of the town's residents to leave Bisbee and relocate elsewhere.

Today, Bisbee is a haven for artists who have settled in the historic buildings and have restored them to their past glory. Bisbee has become a city of diversified yearly events featuring music, crafts, and the arts.

THE COPPER QUEEN HOTEL

The Copper Queen, or "The Queen" Hotel, was constructed by the Copper Queen Mining Company in the early 20th century. With 45 guest rooms, two lobbies, Copper Queen Saloon, patio, swimming pool, and dining room, "The Queen" is Bisbee's major historic landmark. The hotel is a well-preserved Victorian style hotel that is decorated in the manner of the pioneer West. Given the hotel's history of hosting such notables as "Black Jack" Pershing and the young Teddy Roosevelt, it is no wonder that a ghost or two (or three) would find such an inviting hotel perfect for an extended stay.

The following accounts by the hotel's general manager and the front desk clerk will provide further evidence for the existence of "other types" of guests at the Copper Queen Hotel.

CRAIG H. ROTHEN'S STORY

I have been the general manager at the hotel for one year. Prior to working here, I was living in the Phoenix area and working as a hotel and restaurant consultant for a corporation in Northern California.

Not long after beginning my position at the hotel, I began to hear stories from several employees about it being haunted. At the time,

I regarded all of these stories as nothing more than interesting and funny. I personally have never had any experience with ghosts or hauntings. After about six months into my job, I soon changed my mind when I received a call from two guests who were staying in room 309.

The guests were complaining about the room being very cold. I assured them over the house phone that I would move them into a different room. Once moved, they were pleased with the new room. At approximately 9 a.m., I decided to enter room 309, now empty, to find the cause of the cold temperature. Room 309 operates on its own thermostat, and I thought that perhaps the temperature gauge might be broken.

As I entered the room, I immediately felt a chilling cold envelop my body. I walked around the room looking for any open windows. Every window was shut. The air vents were closed, as they should have been. Standing in the middle of the living room, I was at a loss.

Suddenly, the window directly in front of where I was standing opened! I was startled, but not scared. The hotel's windows are not spring loaded so I was most interested in finding out the cause of the window doing what it did.

I walked up to the open window and did not see any unusual wires or loose springs. Attempting to close the window, I placed both hands on the top window frame and began to apply an even downward pressure. I felt, as I pushed down on the frame, an equal amount of pressure from an unseen force pushing up! I actually felt the power of an invisible force that was resisting my effort to close the window.

Just then, I saw movement next to me on my left. I turned and saw the foggy white image of a presence! I let go of the window and moved my hand right inside this hazy cloud. It felt icy cold to the touch.

Now this is when I knew that something was out of the ordinary, I got an eerie feeling that I was not dealing with a normal occurrence. I got the courage to say, "I am going to close the window—*now!*" Once more I placed my hands on the window frame and pushed down. It closed shut easily. I wasted no time in leaving the room.

Just about a month after that incident, late one afternoon, our office had run out of computer paper. I entered the storage closet located on the 4th floor to retrieve some paper. As I made my way out of the storage closet, I heard someone call my name, "Craig, Craig." Thinking I was being called by a co-worker, I answered, "Yes?" There was no answer, and as I looked around, I realized I was alone.

I walked down to the third floor where workers were remodeling a room to ask if they had called for me. The men answered, "No,

"I heard someone call my name..."

we've been busy down here. We haven't taken a break yet." Then they added indifferently, "Mr. Rothen, it must have been the ghost." Not wanting to sound too alarmed by this statement, I answered, "Yes, thank you," and I walked away.

Just in the year that I've been employed at the hotel, I have had employees come to me with their own stories of ghost encounters in the hotel. One of the housekeepers remarked to me that when she was working during the day shift on the third floor, she saw a little boy who was wrapped in a towel appear to her, only to disappear a few seconds later. Another housekeeper reported to me that on the third floor, the doors open and close on their own.

"Howard" looking very dapper in his hat.

The curious thing to me is that the hotel has several log books of reported ghostly activities. These written reports give detailed descriptions of the ghostly events including dates, times, etc. These log books date back over six years. I'll share with you just two short written accounts of what has been recorded. A particular night auditor left the hotel shortly after he wrote the following:

June 8, 1995

I know the ghosts are stirred up again. The phone rang and a gentleman's voice asked for "Howard." I asked Hector, our maintenance man, if he knew who Howard was. Hector had a stunned look on his face. When I listened to the phone once again it was dead. Rose (another employee) who was standing by me said, "It's just Howard checking up on the hotel. Here we go again." *Howard (deceased) was the name of a front desk clerk who worked for the hotel in the year 1910.*

Another employee entry the same night . . .

Guest checked out from the third floor. He was awakened by the presence of a ghost. Also, another guest checked out this morning from the third floor. He said he was awakened at 2 a.m. by a beautiful lady, dressed in black, who disappeared.

LAURIE DOLAND'S STORY

I've worked for the Copper Queen now for almost a year as front desk clerk. My first ghost experience took place just three months ago in June at about 2 a.m. I decided to get a drink of water and walked into the dining room, on my way to the kitchen. As I entered the dining room I saw a strange woman standing against one of the columns. She had reddish brown hair, which she wore up in a bun, brown eyes, and a healthy pink complexion. She was wearing a high collar blouse and was in her mid-twenties.

Immediately I knew this woman was a ghost, since I could only see her body from the waist up! I stood there, startled. I had come upon her so suddenly that the only thing I felt was shock. Eventually, my shock turned to fear. We both stood staring at each other for a few seconds, until by chance, the owner of the hotel walked into the dining room. The ghost woman must not have wanted to stay around because she quickly disappeared! I mentioned what I saw to the owner, but she refused to believe what I told her. Since that time, I have not seen the ghost woman again. I have no idea why she chose to appear to me as she did. However, from time to time I have heard both the footsteps, and the movement of a long, crisp, stiff cloth—like a skirt—as it moved across the dining room floor.

Sometimes at night, I'll be visited by another spirit. I'll be alone at the front office, working at the hotel's computer, when

"As I entered the dining room, I saw a strange woman standing against one of the columns."

I'll suddenly feel the presence of someone walk into the office. I always can tell when this spirit enters the office because the hairs on my arms stand on end, and a thick atmosphere fills the room. I'll begin to get a chilling feeling and soon I'm covered in goose bumps. To date, this has happened about five times.

Fellow male employees have told me about seeing a woman dressed in a black dress who walks up and down the staircase in our lobby. The stairs are located directly in front of the main desk. Interestingly enough, the woman in black chooses to make her appearances only to men. The latest incident with her took place this year, in July, at about 3 a.m. The employee saw the ghost walk down the stairs and enter the dining room. As she walked up to the dining room doors she disappeared! The employee told me that the ghost was dressed in an early 1900s style of dress.

A female employee told me that late one evening when she walked through the dining room, she felt someone grab her shoulder. When she turned around, there was no one there. That was the last time she has ever entered the dining room, day or night!

The sound of a man's heavy shoes walking down the hallways is very common, and one that both guests and employees continually hear in the hotel. I myself have heard this sounds on several occasions. Some nights, in the hotel lobby, I have heard the sounds of unseen people engaged in an uproar of conversation. I can't tell what they are all saying, but they sure do make a ruckus!

Employees always hear their names called out, and when they turn to answer the person they think is calling them, of course there is no one there. This happens so frequently that we all now take it in stride. The ghosts are keeping an eye on us.

Another frequent ghost that employees have witnessed is a young boy who runs up and down the halls of the third floor. We also recently had two guests inform the front desk of a wo-

"The employee saw the ghost walk down the stairs . . ."

man ghost who they saw dressed in a stripper's costume. The guests reported that this strangely dressed woman walked down the hall and opened the doors to the third floor veranda. As the guests followed her, she apparently enjoyed the audience, because she started to do a striptease. The dancing ghost did not last for long. In just a few seconds, she had disappeared!

Guests in room 312 have reported to us strange bell sounds that wake them from their sleep. Once, two women who were staying in room 312 reported that a hat "appeared" to them, floated across the room, and disappeared.

In Room 212, guests have reported "strong winds" that

have rattled the doors and windows and kept them up all night. Once these winds rattled a window to the point that it shattered!

I am convinced that the hotel has ghosts, and I'm not the only one who will admit this. Many employees, both past and present, will say the same. The employees are not shy about describing what they have heard and seen.

I haven't heard of any ghosts in the hotel hurting anyone. I think that when these people were alive many years ago they truly enjoyed the Copper Queen, and they still find it difficult to part from it. As far as I can tell, even death has not changed their strong attachment to the hotel.

"The sound of a man's heavy shoes walking down the hallways is very common..."

THE BISBEE INN

In 1916, owner Mrs. S. P. Bedford constructed a 24-room hotel building which today is named The Bisbee Inn. The hotel was furnished by Mrs. Bedford and then leased to Mrs. Kate La More who renamed it the Hotel La More. Rooms at the hotel were $2 per day or $8 per week. At that time, the hotel was advertised as being "the most modern in Bisbee." Between 1922 and 1923, Mrs. La More's hotel lease reverted back to Mrs. Bedford. Mrs. Bedford operated the hotel under the same name (Hotel La More) until she sold it to Grace V. Waters. Various individuals have since owned the hotel. In 1982 Joy and John Timbers bought the property and partially restored it. Under their ownership, they ran the hotel as The Bisbee Inn Bed and Breakfast. In 1996 the inn was sold to Elissa and Al Strati, who completed the total restoration of the property.

The current inn is a wonderful and romantic bed-and-breakfast. Comprised of 20 guest rooms, eight with private baths, the hotel today is a certified historic property. The original oak and period furnishings, together with the walls decorated with photos and maps of years gone by, reflect the present inn's early days of Victorian elegance.

I interviewed Julie on the front porch of the Inn one warm summer afternoon. My question was direct: "Have you ever been told by guests that there are any ghosts in the Inn?" Julie responded, "Sure, of course, and I'll tell them of my own experiences with ghosts in the building."

JULIE M. CROTEAU'S STORY

I've been working at the Inn as a maid, laundry person, and front desk clerk for just one year. My first experience with the ghost of the Inn took place in January 1996. It was around 5 p.m. and I was in the back lounge where the television room is located. Between the room where I was seated and the dining room were French doors, which were at the time closed.

I noticed movement, and when I turned to look in that direction, I saw a tall man. He was wearing a vest and his jeans were tucked into his high boots. I got the feeling that this was a bizarre guy just by the manner of his dress.

Thinking it was a homeless person who had come in off the street looking for a handout, I said, "I'll be right there." I walked down the hallway to the opposite side of the Inn, through the lobby, and then into the dining room. When I entered the dining room, he was gone. I could not have missed anyone passing me in the hall. I immediately knew something strange was going on.

When I later mentioned my experience to other employees, they surprised me with their responses: "Oh, yeah, that's the ghost of the miner guy."

"What?" I said, "You mean you know who I'm talking about?"

"Oh, sure, his ghost appears to us every now and then."

Apparently, I was not the only person who had experienced this ghost. After that, I didn't want to think too much of it, but I've always kept the experience in the back of my mind. I guess the ghost liked me because of what took place next.

A few nights later, I was in my home, seated on the floor watching television. Suddenly, between my television and heater, I saw the image of the ghost I had seen in the Inn, only this time, he was the size of a large doll! Standing as he was, he was only about three feet tall! I sat there in awe, staring eye-to-eye with this thing. Again he was wearing the same outfit as before. He didn't say anything, but slowly began to disappear.

There is another ghost that other employees have seen. This ghost is of a Chinese man. I don't know much more about him; the employee who has seen the man mentioned the experience to me. I guess she doesn't wish to bring up the subject any more than is necessary.

Sometimes, I'll walk down a hall of the Inn, and spot the movement of a shadow at the end of the hall. By now, I'm getting familiar with these shadows. I know that the eyes can play tricks on a person, but there have been so many incidents that I'm convinced there has got to be more to these experiences than just blurred vision.

All the employees, including myself, have heard doors slamming shut or the banging of metal objects from time to time in the Inn when it is empty. There are cold spots in certain areas of the Inn and one in particular on the stairs. I don't know why this happens, or if there is any rational explanation for these things. I know I've heard these noises and have seen the ghostly shadows. I know that others not familiar with such things might consider me to be odd, but I know that what I've seen is of the paranormal.

I can also tell when something unusual will take place because of a particular flowery scent of lilacs that will permeate the air. It's a pleasant, lingering perfume I've noticed in the air of certain rooms of the Inn. I'll be dusting or simply just passing a room, and suddenly the scent will overwhelm me. The scent will come and then leave after a few minutes. The two rooms of the Inn where I've experienced the scents are rooms 8 and 12. I have mentioned this to my co-workers, and they have responded casually that they have also smelled the scents, and then added "So what's the big deal?"

CHINLE

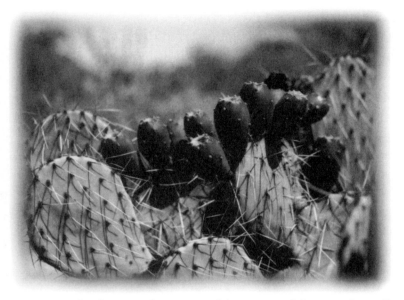

Chinle, near the geographic center of the Navajo Indian Reservation in northeastern Arizona, is at the entrance to Canyon de Chelly National Monument. Chinle became a center for population growth and trade after 1868 when the United States signed a treaty with the Navajos. The first trading post was established in 1882, the first mission in 1904, and the first government school in 1910.

Today the community, at an altitude of 5,082 feet, has been designated one of the major "growth centers" on the Navajo Reservation by the tribal government. It is an important trade, administrative, and educational center within the Chinle Chapter (a local government unit) and is headquarters for the Chinle Agency, one of five Bureau of Indian Affairs administrative jurisdictions on the reservation.

~

I interviewed Josie on the Dineh (Navajo) Reservation not far from the town of Chinle, which is located in the northeast quadrant of the state. Josie is 41, a widow, and mother of twin daughters, aged 16. Our interview took place inside their mobile home, which is situated on deep red, rusty color desert land with wispy juniper trees growing in contorted shapes. Overhead is the endless, vastness of turquoise-blue sky.

This location, with its unique beauty, would be complete if not for the poverty that exists all around. Native Americans daily endure such "inconveniences" as no modern plumbing, electricity, or heating, and diets lacking in fresh vegetables and fruits, but rich in fats, sugar, and white flour, etc. The outcome of such an existence ultimately leads to obesity and other chronic medical conditions, such as diabetes and heart disease.

The interview was conducted in Josie's kitchen. On the table were various small plastic tubes and glass jars containing a rainbow of assorted, tiny, brightly colored glass beads. Josie and her daughters use these beads to make leather hat bands, necklaces, earrings, and bracelets. Once completed, they take these articles to local stores in town and either sell them or exchange them for personal items.

Josie spoke in a calm, even tone when relating her personal experience with a witch and ghosts. Her daughters were in the adjoining living room and silently listened as their mother told her story.

JOSIE'S STORY

My 70-year-old grandfather enjoyed living in the traditional manner of us Navajos in a Navajo roundhouse, or "hogan," which is right next to our mobile home. He also prefers to speak only our native language. After my grandmother's death, he lived alone in his hogan for 20 years. Both he and grandmother had lived together in a previous hogan, but after she died,

Grandfather burned it, as is our tradition when the owner dies. His new hogan was built for Grandfather a short time later, and this is where he now lives.

About eight years ago, in November, Grandfather—who otherwise was in good health—began to suffer from headaches and body aches that eventually caused him to be bedridden. When Grandfather's condition worsened, he began to refuse food. After discussing Grandfather's situation with my older brother, we both decided that it would be best to take him to a doctor in Window Rock. Grandfather was hesitant, but soon realized the logic of our decision to seek medical help. After being admitted into the clinic, he was taken through the long process of many blood tests and x-rays. My brother and I spent three days in Window Rock at a friend's house, while Grandfather was being cared for. When the results of the tests eventually came back from the lab, to our surprise and relief, they indicated that he only had a rise in blood sugar, which could be treated with drugs. Aside from this, his other tests were normal.

However, both my brother and I were not totally convinced that all was well with him. We had seen the turn for the worse, that our otherwise active and mentally alert Grandfather had taken. His state of constant pain and fatigue was very unusual for him. The doctor prescribed pain medicine to help him sleep. After filling the prescriptions, we returned home.

On the return drive home, Grandfather stated that he wanted to seek the help of a local medicine man in Chinle. Grandfather wanted to have a Sing. Among us Navajos, we have a curing ceremony that we call a Sing. The Sing ceremony involves the participation of an elder medicine man or woman. Special songs are sung, incense is burned, and a drum and other ritual items are used. It is a lengthy ceremony and highly respected among traditional Navajos. My brother and I assured my grandfather that we would honor his wishes and contact a medicine man back home.

Arrangements were made with an elderly medicine man, and a date for the Sing was set. Four nights before the ceremony, a strange thing happened to me.

It had been snowing heavily during the day and all that evening. The moon was bright and full. At around 11 p.m., I was awakened by the barking of our dog, who we keep chained to our porch. Usually she barks at skunks that live under the mobile home, or in response to the yelping of coyotes that sometimes come around our property. This time her barking sounded different to me. It made me get out of my warm bed and walk to the window. As I parted the curtains on the front door, I saw a woman whom I did not recognize, walking around my grandfather's hogan. I reached for my jacket and boots, and walked outside.

My dog kept growling and barking. In the moonlit night, I watched this strange woman make her way to the rear of the hogan. When I yelled at her, "What do you want?" She did not respond. I decided to confront this strange woman. With my dog still barking loudly, I quickly made my way to the hogan as my footsteps crunched noisily into the foot-deep snow.

When I was about 20 feet away from the woman, I saw that she was wrapped in a dark shawl from head to toe. Her face was hidden from my sight. Something inside me made me immediately stop in my tracks. As soon as I stopped, the woman suddenly turned away from me. What happened next made my mouth open wide.

The dark woman took off like a flash! She did not run but seemed to float over the snow-covered ground without leaving a trace of footsteps! My dog barked and barked. I turned in the direction of the trailer, and ran back. I missed a step and remember taking a hard fall. Once I reached the trailer I rushed inside and locked the door! Both my daughters told me that they had witnessed the whole affair from the safety of the mobile home window. I was out of breath and shaking. I knew that I had seen something evil outside. My girls were also shaken, and that night we all slept together.

The next day I wasted no time in telling my experience to my brother. After hearing my story, he knew that what had taken place that night had to be witchcraft. A ghost or witch had for some reason visited our home. My brother said, "Who knows how long these evil visits have been going on without us being aware of them?" We all decided that it would be best not to tell our grandfather for fear that such information would upset him. We didn't want to risk him becoming even more ill.

We also knew that this new information needed to be related to the medicine man. My brother drove me to the medicine man's home, and we informed him of what I had seen. He was not surprised by my story. He said, "Oh, I know who this is." Then he explained to us that there was a Navajo medicine woman who lived not far from his house who wanted to gain the reputation in the Indian community as being a powerful spiritual person.

After I heard the medicine man's description of this woman, I could recall her from a visit she had made to my grandfather's hogan several weeks before Grandfather became ill. I remember Grandfather telling me that this woman had visited him because she wanted him to be her boyfriend. When Grandfather refused, she got very angry at him and yelled obscenities. She left our property in a rage!

The medicine man further explained, "It is difficult to gain power without earning it in the correct manner. This woman has decided to seek the help of certain animal spirits instead of asking the Creator for direction, and doing what is right." He also said, "You need to know that this woman wants to hurt your grandfather. Your grandfather refused to do what she demanded, so now she has taken revenge. She chose to make him ill, but she will not stop until he is dead." My brother and I could not understand why this medicine woman would want to be so evil as to hurt our grandfather. Our concern now was for our grandfather to be healed. The medicine man said that he would be ready to confront this woman's witchcraft during Grandfather's Sing.

The night of the ceremony came and we all gathered inside my grandfather's hogan. We used kerosene lamps for light, and a fire was started in the wood stove. Soon the medicine man arrived and the ceremony began. Grandfather was seated on a blanket placed on the dirt floor. In front of him, the medicine man placed the items that would be used for the "cleansing:" A bowl of water, a leather bag of corn pollen, a basket that held a beautiful eagle feather, and various other items. The medicine man began to drum and sing his songs, calling the positive forces of Mother Earth and the four directions. He sang towards the heavens and asked the Creator for vision, help, and power in defeating all evil. His singing continued for about an hour or so. He reached for the basket that held the eagle feather and grabbed hold of the feather's stem. Saying a prayer, he passed the feather over Grandfather's head and body. Then, the medicine man returned the feather to the basket and closed his eyes.

All our eyes were focused on the medicine man's face as it

began to slowly change. His eyes closed tightly, and his mouth twisted, until his expression was one of severe pain. His clenched teeth were very noticeable in the warm orange glow of the lanterns. I held on to my brother's arm so strongly that I know must have left bruise marks. I was scared from watching what was taking place before us. This small, elderly old man seated on the ground before us was changing into something "spiritual." A force had taken over him and what we were seeing was scaring me. Grandfather was so weak with illness that I had to brace his body with one hand so he wouldn't fall over. As Grandfather closed his eyes and prayed silently, he was unaware of the transformation that was taking place in the medicine man.

With a quick motion, the medicine man suddenly turned over on all fours, and with the gestures of a determined dog or wolf, began to crawl around, sniffing the air and pawing at the ground! He then crawled his way to a corner of the hogan and began to dig vigorously with his bare hands at the dirt floor. His breathing became loud and filled with energy. He dug and dug with the force of a man much younger and stronger than he.

I took a quick glance at my brother. His face showed that he was also in awe at what was taking place. I returned my eyes to the medicine man who had now dug a hole about a foot deep. Then he stopped his digging and seemed to recover from his "trance." In a dazed voice, the medicine man asked my brother to bring a lamp over to him, which he quickly did. Then, the medicine man reached into the hole he had just dug, and to all our amazement, pulled out a soil-covered sweater that belonged to my grandfather!

The medicine man stated, "Here is what the witch used for her evil medicine against your grandfather, but now I will use it against her. She used this sweater as her only way to witch him. She will no longer be able to have control over him!" After saying this, he sang a song while placing the eagle feather and corn pollen over the head and shoulders of my grandfather. My grandfather took a deep breath and fell to one side. My brother was ready to catch him as he fell. Grandfather must have gone through a lot of effort, because he said that he was tired and wanted to sleep. We left him there in his hogan covered in warm wool blankets. The ceremony was over.

We followed the medicine man outside the hogan as he carried the sweater and placed it on the ground. He asked for a lamp, and then emptied the kerosene from the lamp over the sweater. He lit a match and tossed it upon the sweater. The fire slowly began to burn and consumed it. Suddenly, in the distance, we heard a piercing loud scream or howl. We turned in the direction of the sound and I spotted a ball of light that rose up high into the sky, and then bounced away into the desert! The medicine man informed us that what we had just heard and seen was the witch. "She will never be able to recover her strength. I found her power, and she will be eaten up by her own evil."

After that night, Grandfather returned to his old self. I am convinced of the powers that some bad people can use to harm others. So much jealously and evil exists in the world. However, it is good to know that in the end, the power of the Creator always wins. I have seen it.

Chino Valley

Chino Valley is the site of the first territorial capital of Arizona. The capital moved to Prescott, 15 miles away, in 1864. U.S. Army Cavalry Lt. Amiel W. Whipple, while traveling through the area in 1854, gave the community its name. "Chino" is the Mexican name for the abundant curly grama grass growing in the area.

In 1895, a narrow-gauge branch of the United Verde and Pacific Railroad to Jerome, joining the Prescott and Arizona Central, was completed, and Jerome Junction was established. Between 1900 and 1925, the activities of Jerome Junction were absorbed by Chino Valley.

The town is in north central Arizona, on Arizona 89, 15 miles north of Prescott and 35 miles south of Ash Fork, which is on Interstate 40. It was incorporated in 1970 and is at an elevation of 4,750 feet.

The economy of Chino Valley is based on a mixture of retail, commercial, and government activities. With the significant growth in Chino Valley, employment has been created in construction, service, and supplies. Agriculture is also a viable business.

~

My interview with Lisa and her partner of 33 years, Geri, took place in their home, 20 miles south of Chino Valley in the nearby town of Prescott. The women purchased the house and 15 acres in Chino Valley in 1962 from a woman who had lived in the house for only three months. Lisa and Geri were attending a party in Phoenix, and by chance, happened to meet the seller of the property. As their conversation progressed, the seller informed Lisa and Geri about the home. That night Lisa and Geri made arrangements to meet her at the property the next day. They drove 150 miles north to Chino Valley and immediately fell in love with the old two-story house and surrounding land.

What now follows is both women's story of an incredible ghostly experience. I don't believe many people would choose to remain in such a negative house unless they had to. What happened to Lisa and Geri in their home is a testament to their strong will to conquer what evil existed in the house. Did they eventually overcome this evil presence?

LISA AND GERI'S STORY
Lisa's Explanation

After buying the property, Geri and I immediately went to work. With a hammer in each hand and the will to make a home out of a real "fixer-upper" we set our goal to start with the most important rooms: the kitchen and bathroom. The bedrooms were next, followed by the living room and dining room. We decided to leave the outside of the house to last. The roof had been patched six years before with hot tar, so we felt it could withstand the elements for another year or two.

We spent the days in our new house, hard at work. Our evenings were spent in a beat-up old trailer we had bought and parked on the property. It was nice to have the trailer to relax in after a day of dust and sweat. Eventually, the kitchen was completed, and in a few days, so was the bathroom. The two upstairs bedrooms were next. Strange things began to happen to both of us after we decided one day to tackle the bedrooms.

One morning, after breakfast, I left Geri at the kitchen table reading the paper as I walked up the short flight of stairs to the second floor. As I reached the top floor, the door in one of the bedrooms slammed shut with a loud bang. The noise was loud enough to startle one of our small dogs. He ran right up the stairs and up to the door where he excitedly barked and barked.

Geri, who was in the kitchen, called out to me, "Hey, what's going on up there?"

I answered, "Nothing, the wind just blew the door shut."

Geri called to our dog, who was still upstairs with me, and as he ran down the stairs, I approached the door and reached for the knob. I turned the knob and pushed on the door to open it. I heard the clicking sound that the knob made, but it would not open. I thought it might have gotten stuck from the force of the slam, so I played with it for a second or two. I managed to open it about an inch, then it came flying right back to its closed position. I had the feeling that something was not right. I called to Geri, "Get up here right now!" I told her that I thought someone was in the bedroom. We readied ourselves for the possibility of encountering a prowler. Again, I turned the knob and pushed on the door. This time it gave a little and with Geri's help, it opened.

We entered the bedroom and immediately felt a cold chill. An overwhelming feeling of what I can only describe as a heaviness or thickness hung in the atmosphere of the room. Geri said, "Let's get the hell out of here!" We both rushed down the stairs and into the kitchen. Noticing our excitement, our two little dogs barked like crazy animals. Needless to say, we decided to leave the cleaning of the bedrooms for another day. The memory of what had happened to us that morning stayed with us throughout the day.

That evening we were having our dinner, once again sitting at the kitchen table. Our only form of entertainment at the time was the radio, which was plugged into one of the few working electrical outlets in the house, in the living room. Suddenly, our dogs began to bark. Above our heads on the second floor, Geri and I heard the hurried footsteps of someone suddenly running from one end of the bedroom to the other. We looked at each other and froze! Between the footsteps, the barking dogs and the music on the radio, our senses became overloaded. We were scared and again concerned that someone might be in the house. Geri stayed in the kitchen while I ran to the trailer. Ready to confront any burglar, I loaded our shotgun and returned to the kitchen.

With the dogs leading the way, Geri and I cautiously walked up the stairs. Geri reached for the light switch, and the single light bulb hanging from wires at the top of the stairs turned on. Our dogs dashed into the same bedroom where we had experienced the negative vibes earlier in the day, then they ran out crying as if someone had hit them. I immediately thought, no S.O.B. was going to hit our dogs. I yelled out, "Hey, we've got a gun, get out of the room now!" The only sound we heard was the sound of our dogs barking behind us. Then I yelled out, "I said, I've got a gun; get out now!" There was no answer. We decided to enter the room anyway.

We soon discovered that there was no one in the bedroom. We checked the closet and opened the closed window and looked outside. No one. We then checked the adjacent bedroom, and again the window was closed shut and it was empty. We were at a loss to explain what was going on.

We sat down at the top of the stairs trying to make sense of something that made no sense. Geri began to cry, and I placed my arm around her. She was really frightened. Just then we heard a hideous laugh, followed once again by the slamming sound of the bedroom door! I got up and pointed the gun at the door, "Get out here I say. Out here now!" The laughter began again and with a courage that even surprised me, I walked to the door and turned the knob and kicked it open. The room was empty! That was enough for us. We took off out of the house and spent the most nervous night we ever had locked in our trailer.

In the comforting light of the morning, we walked out of the trailer and whistled for our dogs. The dogs were nowhere to be seen. They were probably out among the desert brush chasing a skunk or something. I grabbed my gun once again, and we cautiously re-entered the house. It was strange to be walking softly, as though we were visitors in our own house, but we did not want to take any chances. Upstairs nothing seemed strange or out of place. The feeling was a totally different from the frightful night before; everything seemed calm and peaceful.

As the morning progressed into the afternoon, we returned to our normal working routine. When one of our dogs reappeared, Geri became concerned about the whereabouts of our other dog.

After searching for a few minutes, Geri came running to where I was mixing paint. Geri cried, "Come look. I found our other dog, and she's dead!" I followed her inside the house to the living room. There in the corner, where a water pipe was exposed next to the wall, was our little dog. Her head was at an angle, lodged tightly between the wall and the pipe! There was no rational reason for this to have taken place. None at all.

We had to forcefully pull the pipe away from the wall in order to dislodge our poor dog's head. We buried her in the yard and of course, cried for days. Everything was so mysterious to us—the footsteps, the laughter, the slamming doors, the eerie feelings in the bedroom, and now the death of our dog.

The weeks passed, and we did not experience any further strange happenings. The energy and time that we had put into the house was showing. It looked great! We then progressed to the second floor. We started with the farthest bedroom. After that one was completed, we entered the bedroom where we had weeks before experienced the ghostly happenings.

The walls were covered in a very old print wallpaper, which we wanted to immediately remove. There were faded square marks on the wallpaper that showed where picture frames had hung for many years. Geri was going to tackle the removal of the paper, while I scraped the old paint off the window and door. Geri can tell you what she discovered.

Geri's Explanation

As I was tearing away the old wallpaper, I reached a part of the wall about two feet above the floor. I pulled the paper away from this section of the wall and underneath were what appeared to be bloodstains on the wallboard! I called Lisa to look at this and to give me her opinion. She also said that it appeared to be old, dried blood. We got goose bumps. I quickly tore away the rest of the paper. And as soon as Lisa finished mixing the paint, I painted over the wall and the stains. The following day we brought in a bed, dresser, small table, and a lamp. We were done at last!

We had a gathering of friends over one day, who had traveled from Phoenix, who greeted us with house-warming gifts. They loved the house and the decorating we spent so much effort on. Five of our visitors chose not to make the long return drive home that evening, so they decided to spend the night. We stayed up late that night eating, drinking, and enjoying each other's company, in the living room.

Suddenly, we heard a loud crash come from the upstairs bedroom. We ran up the stairs, and when I tried to open the door, I found that it was not opening. Now, with all our friends witnessing, I pushed and pushed. Just as before, I knew that there was someone inside the bedroom pushing against my efforts. I could feel the power of the "person" playing tug-of-war with me. A friend came to my rescue, and with her help we opened the door wide.

We were not ready for the scene of destruction the bedroom was in. The lamp lay broken on the floor, and blankets were all about the room. Strangest of all was the wall by the bed. The blood stains had reappeared! They had come through the newly painted wall!

We all were taken aback by the sight. Our friend said, "Girls, you've got ghosts in this house!" Lisa and I kept quiet, and we knew she was right. With the help of our friends, we cleaned the mess in the bedroom and returned to the living room. Lisa and I informed our friends of the other happenings we had experienced months before. Everyone was shocked to hear our story. As the discussion continued, suddenly from the upstairs came that horrible laugh once again. We all heard it!

Our friend Yolanda let out a scream! We pleaded with everyone to help us solve this thing once and for all. We decided to walk up the stairs and talk to the ghost and ask it to leave the house. There was strength in numbers, so up we went to the bedroom. The bedroom door was wide open. On the bed we had just remade, lay clothes. The pieces of clothes were arranged on the bed in the form of a body! The only thing missing was the actual body. They were neatly placed in such a way as to give us the impression that a body was lying in a coffin! The arms of the shirt were folded at the elbows and crossed over the chest.

I grabbed the clothes and threw them back into the closet. We decided to immediately hold hands and form a circle and pray. We prayed to Jesus to remove this ghost, or ghosts, and to forever cleanse our house of any evil. We took turns asking for blessings and help. Suddenly, in the middle of our "ceremony," we heard the quick footsteps of someone rushing down the stairs and out the kitchen door! We held on to each other's hands with such force. I cried and thanked Jesus for getting rid of the ghost. I knew that would be the end of our hauntings. We all felt so wonderful after that. Thankfully, we have not had any more ghostly things happen to us since that night.

Douglas

Douglas, on the Mexican border, is 118 miles southeast of Tucson, and can be reached via Interstate 10 to U.S. 80. Across the border from Douglas is Agua Prieta in Sonora, Mexico. The Janos Highway, the shortest route to Mexico City and Guadalajara by paved roads from the western United States, begins in Douglas.

Douglas, at an elevation of 3,990 feet, was founded in 1901 as a site for a copper smelter and was incorporated in 1905. Originally, it was an annual round-up spot for ranchers. Agriculture and ranching are still important segments of the area's economy.

~

Our interview took place in the Ryan's wonderfully restored, hundred year old adobe house, which they purchased over 40 years ago. Victoria and her husband, Nandy, currently occupy the house. They have a son, who was raised in the house, but he did not personally experience any ghostly events. Their son currently lives in California and teaches at a state university.

The Ryans, now retired, have furnished their house throughout the years with very old pieces of furniture and folk art from old Mexico. Very early on in their marriage, the "travel bug bit them." Subsequently, through their travels, they've come to know and make many friends.

The house has the appearance of a folk museum, with a wonderful display of very old hand-made wooden furniture and many other works of Mexican folk art—masks, dolls, weavings, etc.

The massive wooden vigas, or beams, that support the ceiling of the house were also brought over from Mexico when the Ryans remodeled their house. The vigas were taken from a church built in the late 1700s in the Mexican state of Chihuahua. The church was abandoned on land that Mexican friends of the Ryans had purchased. Knowing the Ryans might want the hand-carved vigas for their home, the friends in Mexico had the 50 or so vigas trucked to Douglas as a gift to the Ryans. The old vigas can now be viewed in all their antique splendor as they decorate the ceiling overhead.

Aside from the already mentioned vigas and decorations, the whole house has most of the original plank flooring, including the many scratches, knots, and imperfections that add so much to the character of the house. I couldn't help but mention the loud snapping, and creaking sounds the floor made when I walked over it. Victoria responded, "Yes, it takes a little getting used to, doesn't it?" Aside from the annoying floor noises, Victoria and Nandy have experienced quite a lot of other "disturbances" in their home.

I arrived at their house at 4 p.m. and I finished the interview at 10 p.m. Aside from their story of the paranormal, they had many other stories regarding their travels that kept me wide-eyed and hanging on each word they spoke, stories that were incredibly interesting, filled with their adventures.

NANDY AND VICTORIA RYAN'S STORY

As you can see, the house has a lot of special things that we enjoy collecting. It can make some visitors feel overwhelmed. We use that old red *trastero* (dish cabinet) over there against the living room wall to display Victoria's doll collection. It has an interesting story in itself.

When we first noticed weird occurrences taking place in the house, we knew it had to be a ghost. My wife's art supplies began to do some strange things. This might sound crazy, but her brushes moved on their own. We both watched as the brushes lifted themselves out of the metal can and fell onto the table or floor! The brushes rolled a few feet and then came to a stop. We knew that this had to be the work of a ghost. What else could it be? This happened only twice, and Victoria joked that if she could train the ghost to paint on canvas, we would be rich indeed.

The next experience we had took place one November morning, about two months later, in the early morning hours of the night. We both were awakened from our sound sleep by the noise of the floor boards in the living room creaking, as if someone were walking about the house. Thinking it might be a burglar after our collections, I got out of bed and carefully walked to the living room, only to discover that there was not a soul in the house—so to speak.

Victoria also got out of bed, and we inspected every drawer, showcase, and cabinet for missing items. Everything was in its place, except for her paint brushes, which were tossed about the living room floor! We immediately thought that a possum or some other animal might have entered the house and caused all the noise and mess. Our theory soon changed when we began to hear soft laughter in a kind of whispering voice. We both were able to hear this voice and it frightened us. After a few seconds, the laughter slowly went away. "Well," I said to Victoria, "our ghost is back!"

Just three days later, at about 4 p.m., I was in the kitchen making a sandwich when I heard someone say, "Nandy, you stupid man, you are a stupid man, why are you so stupid?" I turned around expecting to see someone, but I was alone, and Victoria was in the front yard watering her apricot tree. I walked out to ask Victoria if she had called me stupid. When I saw her sitting beside the tree pulling out the weeds, well, I knew she would not be so cruel as to call me such names. I told her about what I had heard in the kitchen. With a surprised expression on her face, she told me that the same thing had happened to her earlier that same morning! Not wanting to worry me, she had decided it would be best not to mention it to me.

We had a strong suspicion that things were not going to go very well from then on, especially since the ghost was now speaking to us unkindly. We decided to give the ghost no further attention, hoping that perhaps by ignoring it, it would find some other house to haunt.

That same night, we heard a whispering voice that seemed to be coming from the ceiling above our heads. Try as we could, we were unable to make sense out what the whispering voice was saying. This last episode made us feel annoyed and a little bit scared.

The sound of someone walking about the house was now becoming a regular day-and-night experience for us. Then things really took off. We began to predict when the ghost would want to start trouble, because we would begin to feel a chilling-cold temperature change in the house, even in the month of June when the weather is already quite hot. Once the noises began, the living room always stayed the coldest room in our house. The doors on the old red *trastero* would also quickly open on their own and then be slammed loudly shut by an unseen hand. It was terrible.

The ghost next chose my wife's doll collection to vent its anger on. Apparently, the ghost did not like the dolls because we found them tossed about the living room. One morning we discovered one doll in the toilet, head first.

Another very scary experience with the ghost was when our religious items began to be attacked. In our collection, we have several religious statues from old Mexico, New Mexico, and Guatemala. The statues are placed throughout the house, and we would find them turned to face the wall! We have a small crucifix that I had placed above our bed, which also was turned to face the wall. Once we saw this side of the ghost's anger, well, we said enough is enough and decided to call a local priest for help.

It so happened that the Catholic priest was out of town for a week, so we instead contacted an Episcopalian priest who agreed to bless our house. We were surprised when the priest informed us that given his busy schedule, he would conduct the house blessing the following morning. This was good news for us, but when we returned home our ghost must have known something was about to change, because of what happened next.

As soon as we returned home from our visit with the priest and turned on the lights, I saw a dark figure quickly dash from the living room to the kitchen! Victoria and I had never seen such a thing in the house. Just about an hour later, as we were both seated in the living room watching television, a small clay vase on a side table fell to the floor. Luckily, due to the thick carpet, it didn't break. I picked up the vase and placed it in a box inside a closet. Enough was enough.

We felt that it would be a good idea to light a few white

candles and place them in each room of the house. After doing this, we again sat in the living room and watched television until we felt sleepy. We snuffed out all the candles in the house except for the one in our bedroom. We didn't want to risk having the ghost get so angry that it would want to start a fire.

Throughout the night, we kept hearing footsteps pacing across the the floors of the house. The ghost was apparently upset and was making sure we were well aware of its distress. At one point, we heard a loud "thud" followed by the sound of rocks being dropped on the floor. I got out of bed and walked to each room and saw nothing out of place. I then shouted, "Knock it off, you'll soon be gone from this house, so be still!" After that, I went to bed, and we didn't hear anymore noise.

At 9 a.m. the following morning, there was a knock on the front door. It was the priest. He entered, and I offered him some coffee. Being in a bit of a hurry, he declined my offer and got to the business of ridding the house of our unwelcome ghost.

The ritual of a house blessing did not take longer than a half hour or so. During the ritual nothing unusual happened, except that we kept smelling a strong odor of what I can only describe as iron or sulfur. That was about it. The priest left our home and all appeared to be well.

Victoria and I decided that it would be a good idea to thoroughly clean the house, so we gathered together a mop, broom, and dust pan and got to work. As we carefully moved furniture and rugs, it came time to move the red *trastero*. When I looked underneath the *trastero*, I noticed the floor had a thick layer of wall plaster that must have come loose from the adobe wall. As we each took hold of one end to slide the *trastero* away from the living-room wall, an even larger portion of plaster fell from the wall directly behind it. The thought then hit me: "So this must have been the noise I had heard the night before of dirt or rocks hitting the wooden floor."

In the light of day, we could see that the fallen plaster had been covering a small, wooden-door frame that had been built into the living room wall many years before. We were at a loss to guess why someone would have built such a thing and place it in a wall, and then wall it up with plaster?

We both concluded that the ghostly noises must have been due to whatever this little door represented. I located a small picture of the Virgin of Guadalupe and a small metal crucifix and pinned them to the small door. I then mixed some new plaster and replastered the wall, sealing the religious articles within the wall.

Since that time we have had no further disturbances. Why the ghost was upset, we have no clue. Why it waited all these years to show its anger is still a mystery to us. We are sure glad to have it gone and hope it stays gone!

FLAGSTAFF

Flagstaff, located at the intersection of Interstates 17 and 40, is the largest city and regional center of northern Arizona. It is county seat for Coconino, the second largest U.S. county with 12 million acres. Flagstaff, at 7,000 feet, is one of the highest U.S. cities and its breathtaking backdrop is even higher. The community sits at the base of San Francisco Peaks, Arizona's highest point at 12,633 feet.

Flagstaff is a year-round mecca for visitors. Many Arizonans maintain second homes here. Summer temperatures average 20 degrees cooler than Phoenix (146 miles south on Interstate 17). In the winter there is skiing, ice skating, and hunting.

Flagstaff has long been a transportation hub. Located along an old wagon road to California, Flagstaff was established after the railroad arrived in 1881. Today the town links Interstate 40 to Interstate 17, Arizona 89 to Page and Utah, and Arizona 180 to the Grand Canyon. Historic Route 66 passes through Flagstaff.

Flagstaff's name comes from a tall pine tree that was made

into a flagpole in 1876 to celebrate the Declaration of Independence Centennial.

Flagstaff is a governmental, educational, transportation, cultural, and commercial center. Tourism is a major source of employment. Traditional economic activities continue to employ people.

~

I interviewed husband and wife, Marcus and Ginger, at their home one evening. The LaPortes are a couple in their late 40s who have lived in Flagstaff since 1977. They met and married in the Louisiana city of New Orleans. They now live in a large two-story log home, six miles north of Flagstaff's central district. We sat down for a long comfortable conversation in their living room. The living room has three very large, floor-to-ceiling picture windows, which allowed me to view the beautiful night sky throughout my visit. As their story developed, I soon began to feel a little bit nervous. Needless to say, it was a scary one.

Their story will make the reader pause, and think twice about ever again purchasing "bargain items" at yard sales. What follows is a story that can happen in any state to anyone. The LaPortes simply were a couple who happened to be unaware of anything related to ghosts in their personal lives. As you will now read, such an attitude does not necessarily prevent ghosts from reaching out to touch the living.

MARCUS AND GINGER LAPORTE'S STORY

Marcus and I decided one July weekend to clean out our garage and basement. It is incredible how much "junk" we had stored away throughout the years. We decided that the best thing to do with all the used clothes and odds and ends was to hold a yard sale. We placed an advertisement in the local paper and got to work cleaning out the house. We informed some of our neighbors about the upcoming sale, and word quickly spread around. Marcus also spoke to his mother, who had moved to Flagstaff two years ago. He convinced her that the yard sale would be a great way to sell some of the antiques she had brought from her home town of New Orleans. Although at first she was reluctant to even think of parting with her cherished antiques, she thought about it for a moment and then changed her mind.

The date was set and when the Saturday sale took place we found more "junk" and treasures than we had realized we ever owned. Marcus's mother's antiques were a big hit. A neighbor came by before the 8 a.m. starting time and bought a dresser of mother's. This dresser was not a very pretty piece of furniture at all. It needed some refinishing and the mirror was particularly in need of restoring. However, our neighbor said she "loved it" and she had a space in her guest room where it would look great!

I could tell that Mother LaPorte was very eager to part with this piece of furniture. I asked her why she was so eager to sell the dresser, when just a few days ago she would not even have considered selling any of her antiques. She answered, "Well, I should have gotten rid of that evil thing a long time ago." Her words made me ask what she meant by referring to a piece of furniture as "evil." She responded, "Oh, it's nothing dear, just nothing." I could tell by her voice that she wanted to drop the subject, so I didn't ask her any further questions.

Over all, the sale was a big success, and most of mother's antiques did sell. What remained of the unsold clothes and junk we donated to a local charity. That was the end of that— so we thought.

About a month later, our neighbor who had bought the dresser phoned me and described a very strange thing that had happened to their family. She said that she had removed the dresser from the guest room, and put it in their garage with a carpet draped over it. She started to describe the trouble she and her family had experienced. I was so interested in the little she did say that I asked her to hold her thoughts and come right over to our house. I wanted her to tell her story in the presence of Marcus and his mother. I informed Mother of some of the story which our neighbor had told to me over the phone. Mother responded by saying, "Let's just wait to hear what she has to say." Soon there was a knock on the door and I showed the neighbor in. We sat around the kitchen table and she told the most incredible and scary story I have ever heard.

Our neighbor started her story by saying that after having purchasing the antique dresser from our yard sale, she had dusted it off and placed the dresser in her guest room. "I loved it," she said "I even bought a blue flower vase and a brass brush-and-comb set that I knew would enhance its look. These I placed on top of a white doily on the dresser. It looked beautiful. I also went out and purchased a cute little embroidered boudoir stool and placed it in front of the dresser. It was now complete."

The following weekend, her daughter had come to visit from Phoenix and spent the night in the guest room. During the night, the daughter said that she was awakened by a noise in the room. She slowly opened her eyes and saw that seated at the dresser was a strange blonde-haired woman. The woman was busy brushing her hair. She then noticed that the neighbor's daughter was watching her and turned to face her. In a split second, the blonde woman was standing at the side of her bed!

Her daughter was shocked to see this stranger in her room. She watched as this ghostly woman violently waved her arms above her head. The daughter noticed that the ghost woman was opening her mouth wide and making facial gestures, which gave the impression that the ghost was screaming with hatred or pain but, strangely, made no sounds.

Soon the daughter found the courage to grab her pillow, which she threw at the ghost. Immediately, the image of the ghost woman disappeared. With tear-filled eyes, the daughter turned on the lights and sat on the side of the bed trying to compose herself. She was not sure what had taken place. Did she dream it, or was she visited by an actual ghost? She soon grew tired and leaving the bedroom light on, crawled under the covers and fell back to sleep.

In the morning, the daughter told her mother about what she had experienced the night before, describing it as a nightmare. Our neighbor told us that she was fascinated by her daughter's story, but skeptical. However, our neighbor's skepticism soon ended when they both went up to the dresser and discovered that on the new brush-and-comb set were several strands of blond hair! Since they are Chinese, our neighbor, her husband, and daughter all have quite dark hair. Whose hair was on the brush?

Our neighbor lifted up the brush with the blonde hair strands and showed her daughter. The daughter, very apprehensively stated, "Well, see, now you have the evidence in your hand. I told you there was a woman in this room with me." Our neighbor needed no further explanations. Immediately, she and her daughter removed the dresser from the guest bedroom and placed it in the garage where it was covered with an old carpet. The brush with the blond hair was wrapped within paper towels, placed in a plastic bag, and disposed of in the trash.

Since that night they have not been visited by the ghost, but the neighbor wanted to know if Mother LaPorte would buy back her antique dresser. Marcus's mother said she would, and arrangements were made to place the dresser back in storage. Not once did Mother LaPorte add anything to the neighbor's story. In fact, Mother just sat quietly in her chair listening to the conversation.

After the neighbor had left our house that evening, Marcus's mother surprised us by telling us that she had had a similar visit from the strange blond woman, when the dresser was in her own bedroom, several years ago in New Orleans. She had purchased the dresser from an elderly African-American gentleman. He explained to her that the dresser, among other furniture he was selling at the time, was from an estate sale. Apparently, the furniture and the few other items he was selling were all that remained of a disastrous house fire. Several family members had been burned to death in that fire.

Marcus's mother had her own ghostly experience with the dresser one evening. One night she heard a voice coming from her bedroom. As she walked into the bedroom to investigate, she was surprised to see a strange woman standing by the dresser. The blonde-haired woman stood with her hands raised and clutched together in front of her. She was dressed in a light blue nightgown and had an expression of dread on her face. Marcus's mother asked the woman, "Who are you? How did you get here?" Incredibly, the woman's image immediately disappeared. Marcus's mother had never experienced anything like this before. It was only after she had brought the dresser into the bedroom that the ghost appeared. The dresser must be spiritually associated somehow with its original owner. "I know it's the dresser," she said "I could feel it in my soul that that dresser had something to do with the ghost."

Mother LaPorte wasted no time in removing the dresser from the bedroom to the porch at the rear of the house, where it stood for several years. The ghost of the blonde woman was not seen again until this most recent time in Flagstaff.

The dresser now sits in a Flagstaff storage unit. Who knows where it will eventually end up? For now, the ghost will have to just wait until she can reappear to someone else. Maybe then she'll tell her story instead of just scaring people.

FLORENCE

Florence is in Pinal County, midway between Phoenix and Tucson. Colonel Levi Ruggles, an Indian agent, staked and plotted the town in 1866. Sources cite different origins for the town's name, but all agree it was someone's sister or daughter. By the 1920s, the area had become the agricultural center of the county.

The Florence business district is still on Main Street, and aside from the obvious improvements, downtown looks much as it must have in the 1880s. Both visitors and residents appreciate the diversity of the community. Florence offers the convenience and lifestyle available in a small western community, yet it is only 45 minutes away from the Phoenix and Tucson metropolitan areas. Incorporated in 1908, Florence, at an elevation of 1,493 feet, has been the county seat since its formation in 1875.

~

I interviewed Nancy at her home, located on the far east portion of the city. Nancy is a 50-year-old divorced woman with two teenage boys. Nancy's family is originally from the state of Texas; her parents moved to Florence in the 1930s to work as farm workers in the cotton fields. Her story is about a peculiar uncle named

Edward, or as she referred to him, Uncle Eddie. Uncle Eddie was Nancy's mother's older brother who lived with the Corrales family until his death in 1954.

After divorcing her husband in 1979, Nancy returned to Florence, to the home where she had spent her youth. The house is an old one-story adobe brick house, with a large rusted sheet metal roof. These days Nancy spends her days tending to her rose and vegetable gardens, and some evenings she can be found at the local church bingo. "I live a peaceful life here in Florence. I love my neighbors very much. Everyone is so kind to each other," she said.

Nancy also stated, "My uncle was a really 'special' man. Once you hear my story about him, you'll know why." What follows is my interview with Nancy and her experience with the ghost of Uncle Eddie.

NANCY L. CORRALES'S STORY

Growing up in a small town like Florence was really fortunate for a young girl like me. I enjoyed the freedom and safety of being able to go to the grocery store and not worry about being assaulted. Even though I carried no money, all I was required to do was sign my name on a receipt and at the end of each month, my parents would total up the charges and pay their bill. What bothered me was not being allowed to buy candy— just milk, eggs, and bread.

Sometimes, after returning from work, my Uncle Eddie would accompany me to the store. His favorite thing was to treat me to a candy bar. He would also buy two bottles of beer, which he would take to his friend's house. Uncle Eddie and his friend would both drink their beers while listening to the radio. I know that today this might not seem a very exciting thing to do, but when I was younger, we enjoyed the more simple things in life.

Uncle Eddie had diabetes, and since we did not have much money at the time, he seldom ever visited a doctor. He ate and drank anything he wished and eventually it all caught up with him. One evening, as we were all sitting at the kitchen table, he complained about something clouding his vision. In just a few days he began to see less and less in his right eye, until he totally lost his sight. When he eventually did visit the doctor, the news was bad. He was told that his loss of sight was due to his diabetes.

After losing his sight, Uncle Eddie's personality began to change. He became depressed and spent nights lying awake in his bed. He knew that things could only get worse as the days progressed. He was unable to properly care for his disease, and the result was that his body was seriously suffering. His family and friends attempted many times to help him with his depression, but he knew that his life would be cut short.

I remember the few times I caught him sitting at the side of his bed, and just staring into space. I felt so very sad for my uncle. Soon his right foot became infected, and the infection rapidly spread. He was taken to a Phoenix hospital and when the doctor saw the condition of his foot, he decided to amputate it that very day. So now my uncle was without sight in one eye, and without a right foot. When we returned home with Uncle Eddie, his depression got a lot worse. He now was fully aware of the seriousness of his condition and began to talk about death more and more.

Uncle Eddie called two of his friends over to the house one day, and informed them and my parents what he wished his funeral preparations to be. Thinking back, I know this was a healthy way to look at death and to prepare for it, but I was so very sad to think that my uncle would soon not be with me much longer. Everyone present said that they would do as he wished to fulfill his desires, but one of his wishes really scared us.

He said that he always had had a great fear of being buried alive. He wanted to make sure that he was completely dead when his coffin was lowered into the earth. To make sure of this he wanted to personally speak to the undertaker in Florence and to tell him about his unusual request. Uncle Eddie wrote a letter, which he and the undertaker signed. In the letter, Uncle Eddie had requested that right before his body was to be placed in the coffin, his heart would be pierced with a needle to make sure he was completely dead. This unusual agreement was signed and given to the local doctor, who placed the letter in his medical file.

As the months came and went, we all saw my uncle grow worse, until one morning he did not wake up from his sleep. Uncle Eddie had died that night. The funeral arrangements were made, and just as he had requested, the undertaker pierced his still heart with a needle. The doctor was called to witness and sign his name, thereby stating that the procedure had been completed.

When the funeral and eventual burial took place, it was attended by all my uncle's friends and relatives. We all deeply grieved for my uncle. His death affected me the most, and I fell into a pattern of crying myself to sleep each night with his image on my mind. It was terrible, I really took it hard.

About a month after my uncle's death, my whole family began to experience strange things in our house. My mother was the first person to hear her brother's presence in the house. Early one morning, as she was sitting in the living room, she heard his familiar coughing and sneezing! As she tells it, "I felt that someone was in the living room with me. Then I heard the coughing sound coming from his room. I made the sign of the cross and walked towards my brother's bedroom and right before I entered it, I heard him sneeze! I opened the door, the room was empty. I sat down on his bed and cried and cried." After my mother's experience, I too had my own encounter with my uncle's spirit.

The following night, as I lay asleep in my bed, I suddenly awoke with a feeling of overwhelming urgency. I don't know what this feeling was about, but I lay there in my bed for a few minutes just staring up at the ceiling. Eventually, I decided to go to the bathroom. As I returned to my bedroom, I walked past the living room and froze in my steps. There, sitting on the couch, was my uncle! In the darkness, I clearly saw him as he put on one boot and then another. He must have sensed me watching him because he turned to me and gave me a little wave of his hand. I was filled with fear, and then my eyes filled with tears. I stood in place, then he disappeared. I screamed out, "Uncle Eddie don't go, please don't go!" My parents came to me, and through my tears I tried to tell them what I had just seen. We all broke down and cried that night.

Since that night, we have not experienced anything strange until the following year. On the first anniversary of my uncle's death we held a remembrance rosary-prayer ceremony at the local church. That evening when we returned home from church, we all witnessed the strangest thing. As my family and I were seated at the kitchen table, we noticed that the single light bulb, hanging from an electrical cord in the middle of the kitchen ceiling, began to move! First it swung back and forth, then it began to make small circles. We all stopped our conversation and stared with open mouths at this odd behavior. Then I said, "It's my uncle, I know it's my uncle doing this!" Then the bulb began to immediately make even larger circles. The light and shadows were spinning all around us. We instinctively took hold of each others hands and began to pray.

The bulb began to spin even faster until we could hear it hit against the ceiling with each spin. I was afraid that any second it was going to break. Then just as suddenly as it began its spinning, the bulb came to a complete stop. We all looked at each other as my mother prayed even louder. Each of us knew that the spirit of my uncle had caused this, and when my mother ended her prayer, she asked out loud, "Eddie, please be at peace and go to heaven. We are very scared and want you to have peace. Please go now, please." Nothing else happened that night.

Since then my family and I have not had another ghostly

experience in the house. I personally believe that my uncle wanted to just let us know that he was still around. After mother told him that we wanted him to leave, he felt satisfied and did leave. I don't know what else to think about all of this. I know that my Uncle Eddie did not want to scare us like he did. I just hope he is finally at peace.

GLOBE

Globe, in east central Arizona, has been an important copper mining center for more than a century. Located in a steep canyon, at 3,500 feet, in the Pinal Mountains, Globe is the county seat of Gila County.

Globe was founded as a mining town in 1876 because of its ample water supply and its attractive location for distribution of mining products. The city was incorporated twice prior to its present incorporation in 1907.

More than 20 percent of the employment in Globe is related to mining and the production of copper. Over half of Gila County's sizable manufacturing sector employment is in copper smelting, refining, or rod production. In the area, there are three copper mines, several concentrators, a smelter, and a rod mill. All of Gila County is a designated Enterprise Zone.

The local tourism industry has been enhanced by a $50-million investment by the federal government to provide recreational campgrounds and amenities at nearby Roosevelt Lake.

I interviewed Roxanne, or Roxy, at her ranch, located in a small canyon not far from Roosevelt Lake. Roxanne, her husband, and 46-year-old son have lived in this home all their lives. The house and land belonged to Roxanne's grandparents. Because of the distant location of their home, the Moses family rarely ventures out to town these days. Today, the family farms a few acres of cotton and ranches cattle.

The geography of the land is very dry, with a few groves of trees dotting the landscape. Some of the trees were planted by Roxanne's grandparents, and these can usually be identified by a partially standing wooden fence that meanders near the base of each tree. Years ago, the purpose of this fencing was to discourage the cattle from eating the sapling trees.

On the property are two large barns, several small sheds for tools and supplies, a chicken coop, two corrals, an outhouse (no longer in use), the remains of a collapsed small house that was built at the turn of the century, and the main house.

Roxy has plenty of stories to tell about years past, but it is her story of the strange, ghostly things that she and her family have experienced on the ranch that is most interesting indeed.

ROXANNE MOSES'S STORY

Like my own grandparents, homesteaders came to this part of the state to work in the copper mines and ranch. Many years ago when my own grandparents moved to this area to ranch and raise a family, Globe was just a small developing town. It turned out that fortune was on their side, because on our particular piece of land, two springs were located on the property. While the property was remote, the availability of water was most important at the time.

To the east of the main house that Grandfather built are the remains of the original house of the previous family that had lived here. I don't know anything about those folks except that I understand they had a very hard time making a living.

In the rubble of that house, my grandmother found a broken sewing machine, a small box of odds and ends, and pictures of people she believed were the original owners of the property. Grandfather won the property from the original owner in two card games. I was told that during the first poker game, the owner of the property lost all his money. After losing the first game, Grandfather gave the man the opportunity to win back his loss with another game. This time the stakes were higher. Having run out of money, the man put up his homestead as a wager against Grandfather's wealth of silver and Mexican gold coins. It was with the loss of this last card game that Grandfather won the property. That's how things used to be done in those years. You could walk into a saloon and walk out a rich man or poor man; it all depended on who held the lucky cards.

Grandfather now had a ranch and a bag of money he used to develop the land. My grandparents built the new house and barns, and soon my father was born. During 1917, the first year of my own life, my grandmother died. Grandfather died two years after. I was the only child my parents had. I was quite lucky to have been born; My mother had three miscarriages before me. As an only child, I was spoiled rotten. I didn't have any friends to play with because of the distance between the houses. However, we did go to church every Sunday, and that's when I would get to meet and play with the other children of my own age. The earliest memory I have of ghosts took place when I was a little girl.

I remember one night looking out my window, I spotted mysterious small balls of light that bounced and danced in the distant hills. My parents also saw the lights. Mother and Father told me that the lights were caused by the spirits of the Apaches who used to inhabit the hills and canyons around here. The lights appeared and disappeared at all times of the year. I was never afraid of these lights; we all just accepted them as something normal. To this day the lights can still be seen.

Aside from these lights, there's another, more frightening thing I have seen several times on the ranch. One day, when I was about 19 years old, I was moving three horses from one corral to another. This was during the late morning, just before noon. Suddenly the animals began to act strangely. Something was spooking them to run. I thought that there might be a rattlesnake nearby, or a cougar or something. These hills are filled with snakes, and it is not unusual for them to be found close to the house. One evening I had spotted five of them coiled up next to our front door!

I walked over to the barn and looked everywhere. There wasn't a snake or anything else anywhere. Still, when I tried to corral the horses by moving them through the area, they once again put their ears back—as scared horses do—and refused to pass by the barn. This time, when I glanced over to the opened barn door, I spotted a strange man standing beside the door holding on to a horse's harnesses. I was not familiar with either this man or his horse. I immediately got a weird feeling about them both.

The man was dressed in a peculiar manner, wearing waist-high dark brown trousers, which were held up with thick black leather suspenders. His shirt was grayish in color, and he sported a long thick moustache. I waved to him. He ignored me. Then he and the horse turned around and walked into the barn. I was annoyed by his lack of manners, and walked over to speak to him.

As I entered the barn, the man and horse were nowhere to be found! I thought to myself, "What happened? Was I going crazy?" Then it hit me like a slap on the face. I had just seen a ghost! I ran out of that barn so fast, I must have flown like a bird! I tell you I was scared! When I got inside the house, I told my mother about the ghost. I was so excited and went on and on about the ghost. Mother just sat in her chair and listened. Soon, I got a little upset with her calm attitude and asked her why wasn't she as excited as I was? She told me to calm down and to listen to what she had to say.

She said, "Oh, Roxy, I've seen ghosts here several times before. I just haven't told you about them because I didn't want to scare you."

I was so surprised to hear my mother's words. I said to her, "Why, why didn't you trust me enough to tell me about them?"

My mother responded, "Well, because look at how you are reacting to what you just saw. Now how do you think you would have reacted if I had told you about my and your father's experiences?"

I answered, "You mean Father also has seen ghosts?"

"Oh, yes, honey. Several times!" she said. I was too surprised for words. After a few minutes, we went into the living room, and Mother began to tell me her story about her encounter with the ghosts. "You know those old pictures that grandmother found in the old house? Well, I've seen the woman in one of those pictures, and so has your father!"

*"You know those old pictures that grandmother found
in the old house, well . . .*

She said that about the time that I was five years of age,
she had her first encounter with a ghost in the house. We had
all gone to sleep for the night, and sometime after midnight, a
noise awoke her from her sleep. She opened her eyes and saw a
light coming from the living room. Thinking that my father had
left a lamp on, she got out of bed to investigate. As she entered
the living room, she stopped dead in her steps. There standing
at the door that led to my bedroom was a woman whom my
mother did not immediately recognize. The woman must have
been about 60 years old and was wearing a long black dress of
Victorian style. Mother noticed that the woman's hair was
parted in the middle, and pulled back tightly into a large bun.

Suddenly, something within Mother told her that this
woman was a ghost. Even more surprising was when Mother
recognized the woman from pictures she had seen among the
pictures discovered in the collapsed house years before!

Mother said that as soon as she realized who this ghost
was, she raised her hands to her bosom and calmly spoke to the

ghost saying, "I know you are a ghost. Why did you come to our house?" The ghost woman reached for the long silver chain that hung around her neck, at the end of which was a black, flat shiny stone. The ghost did not respond to my mother's question. Instead, the ghost slowly turned her head to one side and gradually began to fade from view.

Slowly, she disappeared completely into thin air! Mother said that instead of being frightened, she was mostly fascinated by actually having seen a real ghost! You would have to know my mother to know why she would have such a reaction. She was not a very timid woman by any definition!

After the ghost disappeared, Mother went into my bedroom and made sure that I was asleep and that no harm had come to me. Satisfied, knowing I was safe, she went back to bed. The following morning she informed my father about her experience. Dad's reaction was disbelief. Mother said, "I don't care what you think. I saw what I saw, and that's good enough for me!" Little did my father know that very soon his disbelief would change.

A few nights after my mother's experience, father was in the barn finishing up with the day's work. It was late, and there was no electricity in the barn, so kerosene lamps were used for light. Father had two lamps lit in the area where he was rubbing a saddle with oil. He said that he heard the sound of footsteps crunching down upon small stones on the dirt floor. The footsteps got closer as they made their way towards him in the darkness.

Thinking it was my mother, he turned to look in the direction of the footsteps. Standing directly a few yards in front of my father, was the same woman whom my mother had described to him just a few nights before! The woman was holding a lit candle. My father—being the brave man that he is—let out a scream and threw the small can of oil he was holding at the ghost! He ran to the house and told my mother about the ghost woman in the barn. But when they both returned to the barn to investigate, they found it empty.

The next morning my father discovered, on the dirt floor in the barn, drops of beeswax, which had dripped in the same area where the woman with her lit candle had been standing! To be sure, this made a quick believer of my father. No more would he doubt the existence of ghosts!

Sadly, both my parents have since died. My son has been the only other person who has had an encounter with a ghost on the property. His experience took place after he had returned home from the army in the late 1970s. One day he was writing a letter as he sat under one of the large trees by the house.

He said that he heard a noise in the tree's branches above him, and as he looked up, a flock of birds came down from the tree and began to fly all about him. This was definitely unusual behavior for birds. The birds actually flew down in a flock. They did not hurt him in any way; they just were flying weirdly all about him.

Being concerned about the birds' reaction, he got up and moved under another tree. The birds flew away towards the hills. Apparently, that was not the end of it, because whatever invisible force had directed the birds, the same force followed my son to this new location.

As he picked up his pen, and again tried to write, suddenly he felt an invisible hand give the side of his face a big slap, and off flew his glasses! At the same time, he heard the sound of a woman's laughter! He looked all around and saw no one. That was enough for him. He walked over to pick up his glasses, and ran quickly over to the center of the yard. His arms were covered in goose bumps! He wanted to get as far away from the trees as possible. He knew there was no rational way to explain what he had just experienced, except to believe that it had to have been a ghost.

Well, to this day we have not had any further experiences

with the ghosts of the man and his horse, or with the woman. We all believe that the ghosts must be of the family who lived here before us. It is clear to my husband and I that the woman we saw is the same person as the one in the old picture. Aside from my own son's experience with the ghost and being slapped, no one else has been attacked. Now that my husband and I are much older, I don't think the ghosts want to be bothering with us seniors. I guess they think that we'll soon be joining them, so why bother.

HOLBROOK

Holbrook is on the banks of the Little Colorado River in north-eastern Arizona's Navajo County, which is high plateau country.

In 1881 railroad tracks were laid in northeastern Arizona, passing through an area known as Horsehead Crossing. The following year, a railroad station was built at Horsehead Crossing and the community's name was changed to Holbrook in honor of Henry Randolph Holbrook, first chief engineer of the Atlantic and Pacific Railroad. The town of Holbrook, at an elevation of 5,080 feet, became the county seat of Navajo County in 1895 and was incorporated in 1917.

Holbrook is an important trade center for northeastern Arizona, ideally located on historic Route 66 and Interstate 40 and at the junction of four major highways. Positioned between the Apache Sitgreaves National Forest to the south and the Navajo and Hopi Indian Reservations to the north, Holbrook's local economy relies heavily on tourism.

The interview for Roger's story took place at a local restaurant. We sat in a booth in the back of this hangout, and after ordering two cups of coffee, the interview began.

Roger is 66, and except for the five years he spent in Vietnam and the two years he spent married to his ex-wife in Arkansas, he has lived in the small town of Holbrook for most of his life. Three years ago, he divorced his ex-wife when he discovered she was already married to another man in Arkansas. As soon as his divorce was finalized, he returned to Arizona and now owns and operates a vending machine company, which services Holbrook and the neighboring towns.

Roger is a man who knows his community very well. He currently lives in a two-bedroom home about three miles outside of town, which gives him the quiet and privacy he said he needs. Roger also enjoys traveling, and on occasion travels a couple hundred miles west, to the city of Las Vegas, Nevada, for a weekend of "slots."

Roger stated, "You know, I've seen a lot of things, but what I experienced with my folks here in Holbrook just about did it for me." What follows is Mr. Bowen's experience with a sad ghost in Holbrook.

ROGER BOWEN'S STORY

My family consisted of my parents and an older sister, who was two years my senior. We lived on five acres just east of town, off Arizona 180. There was nothing really special about our house and property. We were not rich or anything, but because we had some farm animals, and because my father did a little farming, we always had something to eat. Just above the hill from us lived another family. They had three little kids—two boys and a baby girl. I was about 19 years old when this whole ghost thing began.

It started one day when our neighbor's wife came over to our house. At about 4 p.m. there was a knock on our front door. My sister opened it, and there stood the neighbor's wife who we could tell was quite shaken up about something. She asked to speak with my mother. My mother and the woman sat outside on the porch and talked. My sister and I stayed in the house with our ears pressed to the closed front door. We could hear the neighbor explain to my mother how the neighbor's husband, in a drunken rage, had thrown her against a wall in their bedroom. There was more to the story, but it was so long ago that I've forgotten most of what she said. This is when things began to go bad for the neighbors, to the point that things started to get more violent.

Late one evening, there was another knock at our front door. When I opened it, there on our front porch stood the wife, but this time she was holding a bloody towel to her face. Her husband had taken a swing at her and hit her nose. My father drove her to the doctor in town and luckily for her, her nose was not broken. However, it did leave her with nasty-looking black eyes and a swollen face.

I know it might sound strange, but years ago it was not considered neighborly to get involved in a neighbor's personal problems. The last thing my father wanted to do was to have bad blood with a neighbor. So, all my mother could do was comfort the poor woman with words. It was not long after that incident that the worst happened.

I remember the time that my father and I were cleaning out the stall where we milked our cow. After shoveling out all the dirty straw, I asked my father to pass me a fresh bale of straw to spread over the floor of the stall. As my arms reached to take the bale from his hands, right at that second, we heard the gun-

"Mother and sister were outside looking in the direction of our neighbor's house."

shot. We stopped what we were doing and ran to our house. My mother and sister were outside looking in the direction of our neighbor's house. When we reached our house, my mother asked my father if we also had heard the gunshot. As we both began to answer my mother's question, we heard in the distance the neighbors' two young boys crying. We knew then at that instant that something awful had taken place. We all quickly walked to the neighbors' house, increasing our pace as the boys' cries got louder and louder. We didn't know what to expect.

When we entered the front yard, the front door was open wide, and one of the boys was crying out, "My mother is all bloody." Soon after we found the husband sitting on the living room floor holding his younger son and crying to himself. It did not take us long to discover the reason for the sadness. The wife had minutes before taken a shotgun into her bedroom and placed the barrel to her chest and pulled the trigger. Apparently she had had enough of her husband's beatings and had decided that the only way out of her living hell was to end her own life. I cannot begin to describe the blood and smell that hit us when we entered that room!

The authorities soon were called, and the investigation ruled the tragedy a suicide. The father was taken away for questioning and was soon released. In the meantime, my parents had volunteered to care for the children until the father returned.

When he did return, he piled the kids into his car with a few clothes, and off they went to live with his parents. The father never again set foot on his property or home. A few days later, we saw a truck with a trailer drive up to the property. The two men filled the truck bed and trailer with most of the family's furniture. They finished their work in just a few hours, then off they drove. All was over and done with, so we thought.

My mother never really got over her neighbor's death. The memories of that tragic day also weighed heavily on my sister. We were all pretty sad during the months that followed. It was difficult to forget, because each time we went out our door, the neighbor's house was visible just above the hill. Damn, it was sad.

One day, about six months after the tragedy, my curiosity got the better of me, and I decided to take a walk over to the house. I took my dog with me, and slowly walked up the short hill. Reaching the back door, I just stood there staring at the back yard, thinking about the two children that used to play there. I have to admit that I was a bit uncomfortable. It was midday, and the sun was hot and shining bright. I guess the sun gave me the courage to reach for the door knob and slowly turn it until it clicked open.

My dog began to bark as if something was inside the house. This made me nervous, but I opened the door anyway and slowly walked inside. There were clothes and a few toys thrown about. The refrigerator door was left open, and mice had made nests under the kitchen cabinets. Their droppings were everywhere.

Suddenly, I felt a cold chill come over me. My dog took off like a flash! I wanted to do the same, but then I began to feel an unexplainable dizziness take over. I tried to open my mouth and to move my legs, but I was unable to. I fell to the floor, and boy, let me tell you, was I scared! I didn't faint, I just remained on the floor for a few minutes, shaking with such a chill. I finally managed to prop myself upright, when suddenly my eyes were drawn to the bedroom door, which was about 10 feet away.

There in the doorway was the figure of a person! I was not able to make out any details of a woman or man, but I knew it was a person. I was so scared. I tried to

"Something was inside the house"

move, but I just could not do it. As I watched the figure, it became clearer and clearer that it was the ghost of the wife. I called out to her, "Please don't hurt me. I'm sorry! Please don't hurt me!" Her staring eyes never left me. She just stared as if waiting for me to make a move or to say something more. I sat in that position crying loudly. Then, adjusting her position from one foot to the other, she turned her body away from me and walked into the bedroom.

As soon as she had disappeared from my view, I found the strength to rise from my seated position and get out of that house! I can remember that day very clearly. I'll never forget it, never! I've only told a few people about this. Some people just don't believe that such a thing could actually happen. I don't know how to prove this.

I hope that poor woman is finally resting in her grave, and that her ghost stays with the Lord. I don't think it should be mingling with the living. You know what they say: "A person who dies by his or her own hands will never find rest."

THE NAVAJO COUNTY COURTHOUSE

This historic courthouse is located at the northeast corner of Arizona Street and Navajo Boulevard. Currently within its walls are located the Chamber of Commerce offices and the Historical Society Museum. In 1976 a new governmental center was established south of the city. All county offices were then moved from the courthouse to this new location. In 1981 the County Board of Supervisors requested that the Navajo County Historical Society open a museum in the old building. Local residents graciously donated furniture, keepsakes, and other wonderful items along with written family histories to include in the displays, which are currently on view in the museum.

Aside from the many notorious trials that were held in the courtroom, only one hanging took place, in the courtyard on January 8, 1900, at 2 p.m. The name of the executed was George Smiley, who was hung for the murder of T. J. McSweeney.

Holbrook, Arizona Dec. 1st 1899

Mr. L. B. Perryhill

You are hereby cordially invited to attend the hanging of one

George Smiley, Murderer.

His soul will be swung into eternity on Dec 8, 1899 at 2 o'clock, p. m., sharp.

Latest improved methods in the art of scientific strangulation will be employed and everything possible will be done to make the proceedings cheerful and the execution a success.

F. J. WATTRON.
Sheriff of Navajo County.

Invitations to the hanging of George Smiley, for murder, which occurred in Holbrook on January 8, 1900. Issued by F. J. Wattron, Sheriff of Navajo County.

(above) The first invitation, the news of which was sent out by the Associated Press, brought a letter of condemnation from then President William McKinley to Governor Nathan Oakes Murphy, of the Territory of Arizona. Governor Murphy severely rebuked Sheriff Wattron, and issued a stay of execution, whereupon the Sheriff sent out the second sarcastic invitation(at right)

Revised Statutes of Arizona, Penal Code, Title X., Section 1849, Page 807, makes it obligatory on Sheriff to issue invitations to executions, form (unfortunately) not prescribed.

Holbrook, Arizona, Jan. 5th, 1900.

Mr. A. B. Perryhill

With feelings of profound sorrow and regret, I hereby invite you to attend and witness the private, decent and humane execution of a human being; name, George Smiley; crime, murder.

The said George Smiley will be executed on January 8, 1900, at 2 o'clock p. m.

You are expected to deport yourself in a respectful manner, and any "flippant" or "unseemly" language or conduct on your part will not be allowed. Conduct, on anyone's part, bordering on ribaldry and tending to mar the solemnity of the occasion will not be tolerated.

F. J. WATTRON,
Sheriff of Navajo County.

I would suggest that a committee, consisting of Governor Murphy, Editors Dunbar, Randolph and Hull, wait on our next legislature and have a form of invitation to executions embodied in our laws.

I interviewed Marita at the courthouse, where she is currently employed as receptionist and information clerk for the Museum and Chamber of Commerce. Marita is a Navajo woman who has had numerous encounters with ghosts at the courthouse. She believes that perhaps one of the spirits that follows her around the property is the ghost of the executed man Smiley. "I know he's around here all the time, I can feel him looking at me."

What follows is a detailed account of something that cannot be contained behind glass cases or roped off in rooms. When the lights are turned off at the Navajo County Courthouse and all daily business has ended, another type of activity begins to stir, an activity of curiously weird noises, voices, and more.

Marita can tell you what she has experienced, but of course the true challenge is to experience these eerie events for yourself. The museum's hours are 8 a.m. to 5 p.m.

MARITA R. KEAMS'S STORY

I've been working at the courthouse for three years, and before that I was working at the Petrified Forest National Park gift shop. I have had numerous experiences with the ghosts in the building, and I also know of others who have experienced strange things firsthand.

My experiences gave me the impression that I was not welcomed in the building. I guess I was being tested. Being a Navajo, we are taught that if you keep any possessions of the deceased—a shirt, furniture, or whatever—the spirit of the dead person will attach itself to the item, and you might have some trouble on your hands.

In the museum, there are lots of items of the past that are displayed in the showcases such as old Native American grinding stones, arrows, clothing, as well as lots of non-Indian items. The museum director has informed me that some of these items that have been securely locked behind glass cases have been strangely found outside of these cases, and placed in other locations by "someone." Our museum's kitchen display seems to attract most of the activity. Utensils and other items are rearranged to fit an unseen person's own whim for order. A museum employee named Jane refuses to open any of the display cases unless someone is with her. She keeps her own experiences to herself. Interestingly enough, our own museum director is hesitant to be alone in the building.

All our employees have experienced our names being called out from the second floor. In my case, I heard a friendly female voice, but others have heard both male and female voices calling them when they are alone in the courthouse. Another employee who was the city's tourism director in the past had quite an experience of his own.

His experience happened while he and his family were driving past the courthouse one night. As they drove by the museum, he noticed that the lights had been left on on the second floor, when they should have been turned off. He drove his car to the rear of the building and informed his wife and teenage son that he would return after finding out who was in the courthouse at such a late hour. He opened the back door and just as he was about to enter, his wife called out to him from the car that there was a woman on the stairs on the second floor landing, looking out the window at them. He returned to the car, and sure enough, there was a woman whom he did not recognize staring at them. He, his wife, and son entered the building and searched for the strange woman. Although they did a thorough search, they never found her.

Just a few months after I began working here, a group of kids took a Ouija board up to the third floor on a Halloween night, and apparently made contact with a ghost of the building. The ghost identified himself as "George." George was the person who was hanged right outside the courthouse in 1900.

I was alone one evening in the courthouse when suddenly, I heard a loud, banging metal sound coming from the second floor. As loud as it was, I was not about to go upstairs by myself and investigate. I just remained where I was, hearing the sound.

"Suddenly, I began to hear the sound of someone walking down the staircase."

The next day, I asked a co-worker about the sound, and he said, "Oh, that happens now and then." I decided not to inquire any further.

Just a few months after my first experience, I was once more in the building after locking up for the day. It was dark, and I was on the second floor standing next to a window. Suddenly, I began to hear the sound of someone walking down the staircase from the third floor approaching the second floor where I was. The doors were locked, and I wasn't sure who this stranger might be. The thought crossed my mind that I could be in danger. As I kept quiet and listened for the footsteps, I noticed that they had stopped.

Trying to be as quiet as possible, I listened for any sound at all. There was no further noise coming from the stairs. I convinced myself that perhaps my mind was playing tricks on me—after all, I had heard others speak about the courthouse being haunted. Maybe this was just my crazy imagination. Suddenly, the footsteps started up once more! I carefully made my way to the opened door and peered out, looking onto the staircase. I saw no one. I realized that I must be experiencing something ghostly. I sure didn't want to stay in the building any longer. I quickly walked down the stairs, grabbed my purse and keys, and shot out the front door!

There is another event I have experienced several times during the winter: doors opening and closing on their own. Once I even witnessed the door knob of the front door of the courthouse turn, and then the door open and close. We have double doors that are located directly behind the front desk, which lead out to the rear of the building. I once heard these doors swing open. I walked to the doors to investigate the reason for the noise, and I found that the doors were locked just as I had left them.

"This feeling is strongest in a room where an old chuck wagon is displayed."

Besides my own experiences, public visitors to the court-house have on numerous occasions approached the front desk to tell of experiencing cold chills or the feeling that someone is following them. Just like the visitors, I have also experienced these same feelings. It feels like a cloud of very cold air is passing right through me. I know this sounds strange, but I'm also not the only one that has experienced this. I have been told by visitors that the room where this feeling is strongest is in the room where an old chuck wagon is displayed. I was very surprised to have heard this because that is exactly the room where I have always felt the same thing happen to me.

Another strange, unexplained thing that continues to happen in the courthouse are that the faucets in the men's room seem to be turned on by an invisible hand. At the end of the day,

I thoroughly check every corner of the courthouse, making sure that everything is as it is supposed to be. There have been several instances when I'll return after checking the men's room and find that the faucets have been turned on. I don't know who could have done this, Since I am the only person in the building. I have a suspicion that it is the ghost of "George."

I remember another day when I was seated at the front desk, and the greeting card rack began to turn. It then abruptly stopped. I thought that there might be a small child behind it who was having fun spinning the rack. I rose from my chair and walked over to have a closer look; there was no one near it!

There was a time when for several nights after leaving the building, I would feel the presence of someone following me to the parking lot and into my car. I felt the usual cold chills, and this presence would not leave me. I would even take frequent glances at my rearview mirror hoping to spot something in the back seat.

At other times, I'll feel the invisible hand of someone playing with my hair. I have felt my body being touched so many times that I chose not to discuss this with anyone anymore. They might think I'm crazy. There are times when I'll be so annoyed with George's behavior that I'll yell out, "George, please stop doing this!" I won't experience any more activity for several days afterward, so I know he is paying attention to my anger.

Once we had a man come to us as a volunteer. This guy

was ordered by the traffic court to do community work at the museum as a part of his sentence. Our employees' first impression of this volunteer was not a very positive one. This guy had heard some of the stories about our ghosts, and when he arrived for work, he began to make fun of George and openly stated that he was not afraid of ghosts. We didn't trust this worker and didn't want to leave him alone in the building unsupervised. In the museum, we have a donation box and a few small, valuable things in the gift shop that would not be very difficult to steal. Well, one day I asked him to bring me some brochures from the rear of the building, where the old jail cells are located. We now use these original cells as storage areas for office supplies. Just a few seconds after he left, I heard him scream. He came running to me, saying that the bars and metal were making loud noises and the ghosts were trying to get him. I just smiled and giggled when he told me this. I knew that "our George" was keeping an eye on this guy.

The following is the deposition of T. J. McSweeney after he had been shot. Filed on October 4, 1899.

Question: What is your name?

Answer: T. J. McSweeney.

Question: Where do you reside?

Answer: Have been residing at Dennison.

Question: You are employed as section foreman of the Santa Fe Pacific Railroad Company at Dennison?

Answer: Yes, sir, at Dennison.

Question: What is the man's name who did the shooting?

Answer: George Smiley.

Question: What do you think caused him to commit this act? What were his reasons?

Answer: He claimed I ought to give him his time check when he quit. I had to go to El Paso to have my wife's eyes treated and I asked Mr. Crowley to send a man down there and this fellow worked one day for Garrity and then quit and then, of course, Garrity was the man to give him his time check. I had no more to do with it.

Question: He worked for Mr. Garrity after you had taken leave?

Answer: Yes, sir.

Question: Go ahead and tell me just what he said.

Answer: He just walked right up to me and either said, "Give me my time check" or "I want my time check," but before I had a chance to reply, he came right up and struck me.

Question: What did he strike you with?

Answer: I do not know; something hard.

Question: Where did he hit you?

Answer: In the mouth and face; just one blow.

Question: What did you do then?

Answer: I started to run and he shot me in the back and I kept running.

Jerome

Jerome was once a roaring mining town with 15,000 people and multi-storied buildings and fine homes. It was incorporated in 1899, but with the fall of copper prices and the closing of the Phelps Dodge Mine in 1953, it became the world's largest "ghost city."

In the foothills of central Arizona's Verde Valley, surrounded by the Prescott National Forest, the town is at an altitude of 5,248 feet.

Jerome produced over a billion dollars worth of copper, gold, silver, and zinc in its 70-year active life. Today, life is quite different. The town was designated a National Historical Landmark in 1967. Its economy is now based on tourism and recreation. Antique, craft and gift shops, small boutiques, and art galleries are located in the once-deserted stores along Main Street. Jerome also has one of Arizona's oldest saloon-style bars.

Jerome State Historic Park, "down the hill" from the center of town, features the former Douglas Mansion that has been converted into a museum with exhibits on the area's history. Jerome Historical Society Mine Museum, on Main Street, exhibits ore collections and mining equipment of the past. The annual Paso De Casas (Home Tour) celebrations are held the third weekend in May. Other attractions include Traveling Jail, Gold King Mine, Big Pit, and United Verde Extension Mines.

HISTORY OF THE SPIRIT ROOM

The Conner building was constructed in 1898. The bar was smaller than it is today and, when built, a portion of the bar was used as the lobby for the rented rooms on the top floor. The local prostitutes, or "soiled doves" of the evening, did not use the rooms for their "profession" because the rooms were too expensive. At the west end of the building was a false storefront that opened into a alleyway known as "husband's alley." This became the area where the "working girls" would ply their vocation. Today, that area is long gone.

The bar as well has gone through some changes. At one time it was a smoke shop, then a restaurant, then a freight office, and today, once more, a bar renamed, "The Spirit Room."

PAUL MILVSKI'S STORY

I have been the owner of the The Spirit Room bar for five years. For a time, I lived in Seattle, Washington. I owned a civil engineering firm, which I grew tired of. I had been visiting Jerome for some 15 years, and one day, when the bar was put up for sale, the thought hit me to purchase it. So I did.

When I first moved to Jerome, I rented a room upstairs in room number 2.

I lived there for a few months before I actually opened the bar. People in town had their stories about ghosts being in the building. They even came forward to explain to me what they had seen and felt. Some even said that they had been touched by the ghosts of the building! I was told to be on the lookout for the ghost of a woman in room number 1. Apparently, there is a woman in a red dress who appears to people. The room is located directly above the main entrance to the bar. When she appears, she just stands there looking at you without making a sound and then slowly disappears.

"...he painted the image of the ghost woman in a red dress that kept appearing to him in his dreams."

An artist who once stayed in room number 1 painted the large mural that can be seen today above the bar. He said that he painted the image of the ghost woman in a red dress that kept appearing to him in his dreams.

I've also been told that room number 5 is sometimes filled with "strange goings on." In that room people might experience temperature differences, hot and cold spots, the hair on their arms standing straight up, etc.

I have heard cracking sounds and other such noises on the second floor that have kept me up all night. I have also experienced what I would call "odd, strange feelings" in the building. Other than that, I have not personally had anything else happen to me. Haven't seen a thing. Honest, nothing more. Yep, that's it, nothing else. Not a thing.

HISTORY OF THE GRAND HOTEL

The Jerome Grand Hotel, a National Historic Landmark, was built in 1926. Formerly the United Verde Hospital, it opened in January 1927 and was one of the most modern hospitals in the Western States. It served the Town of Jerome and the surrounding communities until its closing in 1950. The Hospital was kept in standby condition—fully furnished, equipped, and ready to reopen, if needed until the 1970s. It was purchased in 1994 from the Phelps Dodge Mining Company to be historically renovated and reopened as Van Alan's Jerome Grand Hotel in 1996.

Despite more than three years of renovation, the building has maintained over 95 percent of its original integrity. The Otis elevator is once again providing service to all five levels, and heat for the hotel is provided by the original Kewanee boiler system installed in 1926.

As one of the highest public buildings in the Verde Valley,

(elevation 5,260 feet), Panoramic views of the San Francisco Peaks, the Red Rocks of Sedona, and the entire Verde Valley are breathtaking. The hotel is located within walking distance of downtown Jerome.

Along with the hotel and gift shop, the historically renovated 1920's style lounge and restaurant are now open, making the Jerome Grand Hotel the only full-service hotel in Jerome in more than 40 years.

THE DEATH OF CLAUDE M. HARVEY

On April 4, 1935, *The Prescott Evening Courier* reported that Claude M. Harvey, an employee of the United Verde Hospital and a well-known resident of Jerome, was instantly killed in the basement of the hospital. The man's unavoidable death was caused when his head was pinned under the elevator. Further, there were no eyewitnesses to the tragedy.

Born in Scotland on February 20, 1872, Mr. Harvey had been employed as the hospital's fireman engineer from 1932 until his death. Mr. Harvey was known to the community of Jerome simply as "Scotty" or "Dad."

John Zivkovich, a hospital employee, discovered the body. Dr. M. S. Meade examined the body, and Mr. T. C. Henson, electrical engineer, removed Mr. Harvey's body from the accident scene and testified that the elevator was in perfect working order.

Given all the testimonies following the death, presented to the coroner's jury, there were many individuals, then as now, who believe that Scotty Harvey was murdered. Various theories of the possible crime exist among present employees of the hotel and townsfolk. These circulated stories lead the listener to wonder if Scotty's ghost is not yet resting in peace. Could the shadowy figure of a short man, seen darting about the hallways and boiler room of the present hotel, be the ghost of Scotty? Could the presence that is sensed of a man on the second and third floors of the hotel be that same spirit?

ELIN HEARD'S STORY

I'm originally from Wales and am the bar manager of the Grand View Lounge. Prior to working at the hotel, I was told about scary things that had taken place in the building.

My only experience with a ghost took place right here in the bar of the Grand View Lounge. As I was entering the lounge one day, I saw a fellow worker standing behind the bar. Strangely, standing directly behind her was a woman whom I did not recognize. The strange woman was not very old, about in her late 20s. She had long dark hair, pulled back, and was wearing a white blouse with a high collar. Over the blouse, she wore a dark jacket. My impression was that this woman was wearing clothing of a by-gone time.

I soon could tell that this woman did not want me to notice her, because as I began to stare at her, she quickly turned around and went through the doorway into the back storage room of the bar. There is no exit door in the storage room—just one way in and one way out.

I asked the employee, "What the heck is that woman doing here in the bar?"

The employee was perplexed at my question, because she responded with, "What woman? There's no one here." I told her that I had seen this woman standing right behind her and that she had just walked away into the storage room. The employee was speechless because she obviously did not see the woman.

I decided to investigate the storage room. When I did, I found no one in sight. I knew immediately that the strange woman I had just seen was a ghost. I have lived in a lot of places where ghosts are regularly seen. So I guess I accept such things and do not get very excited. I accept them for what they are, and I leave it at that.

I have not heard of other staff or guests seeing this spirit in the lounge. Some people might not wish to tell about such experiences you know. However, one story in particular that I can recall is about a woman guest.

One evening, the woman removed her necklace and earrings and placed them on the table by her bed. After waking in the morning, she reached for her jewelry and discovered that her necklace and earrings had fused together into a clump of melted gold! I have also heard talk of a ghostly little boy, about the age of six or seven, who appears on the third floor. He is seen with a playful grin on his face, and then he disappears.

"She quickly turned around and went through the doorway into the back storage room!"

JENNIFER A. EDENS'S STORY

I've been working at the hotel as the front desk clerk and gift shop cashier for over six months. Prior to working here, I definitely was told about the building being haunted. Growing up in the not-so-distant town of Sedona, local people are well aware of the hotel's ghostly reputation.

I consider myself to be a logical woman, and I have tried to make sense of what I have experienced here. I also know that what I have seen at the hotel is not normal and can't be explained in logical terms.

My personal experiences happened just a few weeks after I

"Sometimes I get the strange feeling that someone is watching me."

started my job. One evening I was alone, working the 4 p.m.-to-midnight shift. I was seated at the phone switchboard when I heard noises coming from the gift shop area. I got up from my chair and went to investigate. I saw that several items, which I had securely placed on the gift-shop shelves, were now on the floor. An unseen force of some kind was actually tossing small dolls and other bric-a-brac off the shelves! The items that I had personally placed on the shelves went flying! Then everything stopped. I have not had this happen since.

Once, I arranged the chairs in the sitting area directly in front of my desk, then turned my back. Moments later, they had been returned to their original position by an unseen hand. I know this might seem nutty, but I am the only person in the room, and this really does happen.

At night when I am seated behind the desk reading a book, I sometimes get the strange feeling that someone is watching me. I can "feel" the glaring eyes of a man staring at me from the stairs just a few feet away. Once, when this feeling became too overpowering, I quickly turned my head and looked toward the stairs. As I did this, I got a glimpse of the shadowy figure of a man! He stood still and then walked up the stairs and out of my sight. That shook me up a bit. I was quite alert throughout the rest of the night.

You might have heard about the employee, Mr. Harvey, who once worked at the building and who committed suicide? Some say he was murdered. Well, they found his body at the bottom of the elevator shaft, which is just a few feet away from my working area. That sure gives me a lot of comfort knowing a dead man's body was found over there...

Once, as I walked down to the basement, I entered the boiler room and saw the shadowy figure of a man walking about the room. I didn't think much about this at the time, because I thought it was the manager of the hotel. I soon found out that the same day I was downstairs, the manager was out of town. The thought of encountering that ghost down there alone just sent shivers down my back. Eventually, the word got around about my boiler-room experience, and other staff members came forward to tell me about seeing the same shadowy figure in other areas of the hotel. I know that there has got to be a reason for this ghost appearing to all of us. Could it be the spirit of the man that died here? Who can tell?

I have had another strange thing happen. My switchboard has received calls from rooms that are empty. This switchboard is an old one, but works perfectly fine. I have never had any problem with the system. I began to get these unusual calls from rooms that had been vacated by a guest. Once, when I checked out an elderly couple, from my window, I saw them get into their car and drive off. No sooner had they done this, the switchboard began to ring; the call was coming from the room they had just left. I carefully picked up my receiver and said, "Yes, can I help you?" All I heard was static at the other end. I felt as if someone was playing with me. The thought did cross my mind that perhaps it might be the maid playing a trick on me, but I know the maid and she would not do such a thing. At one time, when the switchboard began to ring in an empty room, the maid walked right past my desk! It couldn't have been the maid because she herself has experienced unusual ghostly things, and I know that she has been so shaken up by these experiences that she would not play around with me like that.

I hope I don't ever see anymore shadows or hear any more noises and ringing phones. I work the evening hours, and I don't need to be shaken when I am all alone.

LAINA R. GALLOWAY'S STORY

I have been working as head housekeeper of the hotel for seven months. I was born in Jerome and moved away for several years before returning. Growing up, I always heard local stories about the hotel being haunted, and one day I personally experienced strange events at the building for myself. As a child, I lived with my family in a home just above the hill from the building that used to be a hospital before the present owners turned it into The Grand Hotel.

Well, one day my sister and I walked down the hill towards the building. Suddenly, we both clearly heard a woman's screams coming from within the abandoned building. The numerous stories that people used to tell were about screams and other noises coming from the old hospital. Now we were hearing them for ourselves. Of course, there could have been someone in the building playing a trick on us, but it all seemed so spontaneous and real at the time. Not wanting to investigate any further, we ran home.

A few days after I began my job at the hotel, I began to hear strange sounds coming from rooms I knew to be empty, the sound of people conversing with each other. Even now I get scared and uneasy when I recall that. My sister, who also works in housekeeping, has also heard the voices in other rooms. Most often we hear them on the third floor, in rooms 31, 33, 39a, and 39b. Those days, I get scared working alone in those rooms.

In one room I saw the strangest thing: a shadow of a man walked right past me! As soon as I entered the room, I began to see a hundred little lights floating around. It was as if they were moving as a group in mid-air, much like a school of fish might behave. The lights really appeared to be like someone had thrown handfuls of sparkles into the air. After a few seconds, they slowly disappeared.

Another time, while in a room, I heard the sound of an old, large cart being wheeled across the hall. I could tell it was an old cart because of the squeaking sounds its metal wheels made. At the time I was using the hotel's only cart, and it was in the room with me. Curiosity got the better of me, so I walked into the hallway to investigate. The hallway was empty. Could that sound be

*"I refuse to go into that room
without someone else being with me."*

the noise of a hospital cart, used years ago when the building was a hospital? Or could it have been a hospital cot being pushed by the ghost of a nurse?

Again, alone in a room, I'll hear my name being called out. I'll turn and face the direction of the voice, and there will be no one. My sister has had this happen to her, but "they" actually scream out her name in her ear. Of course this upsets her, but what can she do?

I'll also have doors slam shut while I'm in a room. There is no wind to cause such a thing to happen, so what would cause closet and room doors to close with such force? Whenever a door slams on me, I loudly say, "Stop it and leave me alone! Can't you see I have to work?" Things will subside for a few days, only to start up again. I would like for the spirits to leave me alone. I have no idea why they enjoy bothering me this way. They seem to be at their most annoying during the day, because everything that I have told you has happened to me only in daylight hours.

One day, as I was vacuuming the third-floor hallway, a shadowy figure came right up to me and brushed against my left side. The shadow was moving quickly, and I had the impression it was that of a man. It also seemed to be threatened and angry, because of the manner in which it pushed me. I was so scared that I dropped what I was doing and dashed out of the room. Because I needed to finish cleaning that room, I located a fellow employee and asked her to accompany me. I refused to go into that room without someone else being with me.

A friend of mine who used to work at the hotel once told me that she had seen the ghost of an old lady. That ghost appeared twice to my friend. There is also a male employee who works the front desk, who on several occasions has seen the ghost of an old woman. He told me that the ghost appears on the stairwell by the elevator, dressed in a white dress.

I also recall an employee who worked for the hotel for just a day. She was hired as a maid, and while she was cleaning a room, she was actually attacked by a ghost! She told me that the ghost grabbed hold of her body and would not let her go! She struggled and struggled, but it held on. The supervisor soon called an ambulance that took her to the hospital. After that experience, she never returned to work.

I do not want to see ghosts anymore! I try to be firm with the ghosts when they start to play tricks on me. I keep telling them to understand that I have to work for a living, that I don't want to be scared. I really don't like to be alone in empty rooms, but what can I do? It's my job. I don't have much choice, do I?

HISTORY OF THE JEROME GRILLE AND INN BUILDING

The Clinkscale building was constructed in 1899 and has been in continuous operation since that time. It originally housed a hardware store on the first floor and offices on the second. Its history is as varied and colorful as the town of Jerome itself. The building is made of poured reinforced concrete, with walls up to 18 inches thick. The original owners wanted the building to be as fireproof as possible, since it had been built on the ashes of the third major fire to have devastated the town within the past 18 months. As documented in the *Jerome Reporter Supplement* of December 28, 1899, this building was the creation of J. G. Clinkscale, a California and Arizona insurance adjuster, as an "ornament to the City."

The Inn at Jerome is an elegantly restored Victorian inn that boasts eight guest rooms, including one named, "Spooks, Ghosts and Goblins." The proprietors have shown great care to detail and have selected all the furnishings with comfort in mind. Genuine goosedown pillows complement each bed, as does memorabilia of the West. A large parlor and fireplace is always available to guests for quiet conversation (perhaps a ghost story or two), and incredible views of the Verde Valley may be seen from the many windows that provide vistas of Sedona's Red Rock County and the mountains of Flagstaff's San Francisco Peaks.

BILLIE JO SHEPHERD'S STORY

I've been working at the Grille as head waitress for about a year, but I've also worked upstairs in the Inn. In fact, the Inn is where I first saw what I would call a ghost. Of course, I was told about the place being haunted, but those stories don't mean much until a person experiences such things firsthand. When my friends found out that I had got the job at the Inn, the first thing I was told was, "Be careful! Don't you bring back any ghosts with you!"

I had been working for only two months when I experienced a ghost. It was about 4 p.m., and I was in the room named "Victorian Rose." Now, this might sound a bit unusual, but I saw the shadow of a man move across the room and then go behind the door! Yes, I was scared, so scared that I ran down the stairs to the first floor! I'm not a superstitious person, but this did frighten me.

Today, I'm working downstairs in the Grille restaurant, but I guess the ghost doesn't care where I work because just last week I had something else happen to me. I was alone in the early morning when I thought I heard the cook walk in. I heard footsteps approach me from behind. I began to speak out loud, thinking that I was talking to the cook. When there was no verbal response, I turned around and there was that same dark figure of a man I had seen upstairs, standing with his head bent to one side. He just stood there looking at me with a cold stare. I let out a loud scream, and then that thing disappeared!

About five minutes later, the cook came in. I told him about what I had just seen, and he paid close attention to my story. After I had finished, he told me about his own experiences with a ghost that rubs against him. You might want to speak to him and get his story. He said that it rubs against him like a large cat would do. Isn't that the strangest thing you ever heard?

JoAnne Chasteen's Story

I've been working at the inn for close to three years as the housekeeper, and I'm originally from Southern California. As soon as I told local friends about my new job, they congratulated me, and then they shared their stories about the building being haunted.

I had my own ghostly encounter one day while I was cleaning a room named "Lariat and Lace." I was feeling uncomfortable as I worked, as if someone was in the room with me, watching every move I made. I couldn't seem to shake this feeling. Then I saw the movement of people's shadows in the room. These shadows moved away from me, and then disappeared!

There have been several other times when I was in a room getting it clean for the next guest's arrival. I do the usual routine things like dusting and making the bed with fresh sheets and pillowcases. After I had made the bed, I would return just a few minutes later and find to my surprise the impression of a person's body on the comforter and pillow! I have no idea how this could happen. Not wanting to leave the bed in such a condition, I would once again fluff the pillow and straighten out the wrinkles on the bed. I knew that a ghost must have been responsible and was playing a game with me. As I turned away for a second or two, the pillow once more would have the same impression! This weird thing has happened to me in two particular rooms, "Kiss and Tell" and "Pillow Talk." I don't necessarily feel frightened when this happens, just annoyed.

I also know that the inn has cold and hot spots; areas where extreme temperature changes are felt for no reason. The staff knows about these things, especially the ones that have been with the inn for several years. I have heard of strange things happening in the kitchen, such as trays of glasses and dishes being thrown to the floor and broken. In the area of the bar, bottles of liquor have also been knocked to the floor and broken.

All in all, I don't think I would like to experience such things any more. I enjoy a quiet and peaceful workplace. I know that upstairs in the Inn, things are peaceful, but downstairs in the Grille, well . . . that's another story.

KINGMAN

Kingman is located in northwestern Arizona at the intersection of Interstate 40 and Hwy. 93. Kingman is situated in the Hualapai Valley, between the Cerbat and Hualapai Mountain Ranges, at an elevation of 3,400 feet. The city was established in the early 1880s by Lewis Kingman, who located the route of the Santa Fe Railway. It was incorporated in 1952 and has served as county seat of Mohave County since 1887.

Kingman is a regional trade, service, and distribution center for northwestern Arizona. Its strategic location relative to the Grand Canyon, Los Angeles, Laughlin, Las Vegas, and Phoenix and has made tourism, manufacturing, distribution, and transportation its leading industries.

～

My interview with the Greers was held in their kitchen while we shared a pizza. The Greers are a wonderful retired couple who have enjoyed living in Kingman since their move from California. Charlie raises gourds in his large backyard, while Ursula paints and decorates them with fancy designs. Their house is filled with these crafts. Several times a year, the Greers box up their decorated gourds, climb into their RV, and tour the United States, selling their goods at flea markets and craft fairs.

The Greer's personal ghost story is as equally unique and as unusual as the Greers themselves.

URSULA AND CHARLIE GREER'S STORY

We've only lived in Kingman for two years. Originally we are both from Los Angeles, California. We decided to leave Los Angeles because of the problems with crime, smog, and everything else that goes along with living in a big city. Basically, we just got tired of the rat race.

We looked all over the state of Arizona and decided on relocating to Kingman because of its location, right on Interstate 40. Yeah, we'd heard all the jokes about how hot the summers can be from our friends back in California. It does get very hot out here, but just like everyone else in Kingman, we've gotten used to scheduling our outdoor activities to start before the sun rises and after it sets. It's not so bad.

The house we bought was built in 1952, so that makes it 44 years old this year. That's not too old as far as houses go, but its old enough for it to be haunted! I guess this is a good place to begin our story about what's been going on here since we moved in.

Charlie and I were only in the house for one night when we heard what sounded like a heavy branch of a tree being blown by the wind against the side of the house, making a scratching sound. We were both asleep, and this noise was loud enough to wake us both up. Charlie got out of bed and took a peek out the bedroom window. He was expecting to see a strong wind blowing sand and trash all about the yard, but it was as still as could be. I thought that perhaps a stray dog or cat had been the cause of the noise, but we didn't see any animals. Soon the noise stopped, and we thought nothing further about it and went right back to sleep.

Well, this did not happen again for a couple of weeks, until one night when I was busy in the living room unpacking a large cardboard box from our move. Charlie had driven into town and was visiting with a friend. Since I was alone in the house, I turned on the radio and tuned it to a country station. A song came on I liked, so I turned up the volume. After turning away from the radio, I took a passing glance at the direction of the kitchen, when I saw who I thought was my husband, Charlie, walk past the doorway. Over the sound of the radio I yelled at Charlie, "Hey, boy, what are you doing back so soon? You trying to scare me sneaking in like that!" Normally Charlie would respond, but this time there was no response. I walked to the kitchen, and there on the table was a man's hat. I stopped in my tracks and again I called out for Charlie. When there was no reply, I went to the door that led out to the backyard. It was locked from the inside!

"There on the table was a man's hat!"

I turned around to look at the hat. It was a dirty brown color, covered with dust, with a wide, old, satin band stained with perspiration. I noticed it had a strong smell of wet earth. I placed it back down on the table, and I immediately got a frightening chill that took over my body. I dashed for the front door yelling, "Charlie, Charlie, where are you?" As I got outside, I went around the back of the house and saw nothing unusual. I decided that I did not want to be in the house alone, so I waited out in the street until I spotted Charlie's car driving towards me in the darkness, about an hour later.

I guess Charlie can explain how I reacted from this point.

Charlie's Explanation:

When I drove up to the house, I was surprised to see Ursula standing in the middle of the street. I parked the car in the driveway, and she came right up to me before I even opened the car door. I got out, and she grabbed me and began to cry. She told me quickly that there was a stranger in our home who had been watching her and that she had probably scared him away, but she was not sure. I opened the trunk of the car and brought out a small steel pipe that I used as an extension handle for a wrench. Armed with this weapon, we entered the house, with me leading the way.

We completely searched each room and found the entire house to be empty. The old hat that Ursula discovered on the kitchen table was nowhere to be found. There was not a trace of anyone in the house other than the two of us.

About a week passed without another incident, but soon Ursula began to have strange dreams. These dreams were very scary even to me. I was awakened by her moaning and screaming. As I turned on the light in our bedroom, I saw that she was covered in sweat. I shook her in order to wake her, and she opened her eyes and whimpered. I knew something was not right. When I asked her to tell me her dreams, she did not want to discuss anything until the next morning. She can tell you what she was dreaming about those nights.

Ursula's Explanation:

All I remember is dreaming of this older man—whom I did not recognize—who approached me with a very painful look on his face. In my dream he is wearing that very same hat that I found that night on the kitchen table. He would take short steps towards me, as though limping. I guess that is what seems to be the most frightening to me, his limping. Then he holds out both arms and takes a strong jump towards me! This is when I begin to scream with all my might, and Charlie wakes me.

One thing that Charlie did not mention was that one night when I was having the same bad dream, he woke me and as I lay there in bed, I told Charlie that my shoulder was hurting. When Charlie turned on the light we saw the red marks of

"He was riding his horse into the Hualapai mountains."

a man's fingers left on my shoulder! Boy, were we scared. I told Charlie, "See, that's what I've been afraid of all along, that that man would grab me!"

Soon after, my bad nightmares stopped, but that was not the end of it. One day I decided to speak to the realtor who had sold us the house. I was a little apprehensive, but I informed her about what Charlie and I had experienced at the house. The realtor said that I should go to the town of Truxton, about 20 miles north of Kingman, and speak with a man named J. B. who was the seller of our house. That very afternoon Charlie and I drove to Truxton and met with J. B. The story he told us really made us believers in the existence of ghosts. This is what J. B. told us:

Many years ago, the original owner of our house, Mr. Altenberry, was riding his horse in the foothills of the Hualapai mountains just south of Kingman. He and a friend were riding on a trail, and everything was going fine until his friend's horse was spooked by a rattlesnake. The horse reared and knocked Mr. Altenberry's friend off.

Well, Mr. Altenberry decided to teach the rattlesnake a lesson, so he dismounted his horse and approached the snake. The

*"He took
hold of the
creature's
tail and held
it up above
his head."*

rattler was a big son-of-a-gun, about a six-footer! Mr. Altenberry used a stick he had found to coax the snake out of from under a bush, and with his friend's help, they used a large rock to kill the poor animal. Apparently, the two men were so overjoyed with their successful hunting skills that they decided to gather up the limp trophy and take it back into Kingman to display to all who wished to listen to their story.

Mr. Altenberry took hold of the creature's tail and held it up above his head for his partner to determine the serpent's actual length. No sooner had he lifted its tail above his head, the once lifeless head quickly turned around and sunk its fangs into his thigh! Boy, were the men surprised!

With all the commotion that was taking place, both horses took off at a gallop, and the two men were left to chase after their horses before going back to town for medical attention. A few hours later, one of the horses was caught, while the other was "spooked real good" and refused to be captured. By this time, the ailing Mr. Altenberry's whole leg was swollen. The snake's toxin was doing its job, and he knew he was in a bad situation.

The two men decided that Mr. Altenberry should ride the one remaining horse into town. Mr. Altenberry was in such a terrible state, he began to shake violently. His friend knew that he would not be able to ride alone, so Mr. Altenberry was left at that spot while his friend rode at a gallop into town for help. Apparently, Mr. Altenberry's friend stated that Mr. Altenberry must have been aware of his terminal fate, as he could hear his friend's screams of pain as he rode into the distance.

Soon a team of men returned to the spot where Mr. Altenberry had last been seen. They found his body sprawled over a boulder. He had known that someone would return for him, so, with the last bit of strength he could muster, he had hung his hat on a top branch of a nearby desert paloverde tree, in the hope that they would spot his hat and locate his body.

Well, that was the story that J. B. told to Charlie and me. We were satisfied with what we now knew and how it related to the limping man in my dreams, the dusty hat in my kitchen, and the man I had spotted walking in my house. I don't want to experience any more visions of the "limping ghost" in the house. We have not heard or seen anything else. I sure hope we don't.

NOGALES

Nogales, Arizona, and its twin city, Nogales in Sonora, Mexico, are on the international border separating the United States from Mexico. The Arizona city serves as both the economic capital and the county seat of Santa Cruz County, the smallest and southernmost of Arizona's counties. The city is in a mountainous setting, at an elevation of 3,865 feet. Nogales was established in 1880 by Jacob and Isaac Isaacson, who built a trading post along the border. Two years later, Nogales was the site of the first rail connection between Mexico and the United States. Nogales incorporated in 1893.

International commerce is an important part of Nogales's economy. Its location makes Nogales a vital retail hub for shoppers from Northern Mexico. More than 40 percent of Nogales's sales tax comes from the 50,000 or more Mexican shoppers who cross the border every day.

Nogales, Arizona and sister city Nogales in Sonora, Mexico, are home to one of the largest cooperative manufacturing (*maquiladora*) clusters along the U.S.–Mexico border.

The *maquiladora* concept uses U.S. manufacturing plants located on both sides of the border to take advantage of favorable
wage and operating costs and excellent transportation and distribution networks.

~

*I interviewed Dorotea at her home early one morning. Dorotea
was not shy about revealing her age of 74. Although she has had
a plentiful life thus far, there have been a few tragedies to overcome. One in particular was the death of her husband many years
ago. Her husband died in a mining accident and left her with a
baby son to raise. Her son also lives nearby.*

*Dorotea surrounds her three-bedroom house with a lov-
ingly-tended garden of hollyhocks and sunflowers and her favorite:
pink rose bushes. Proudly displayed in her home are photos of her
husband, son, and grandchildren.*

*At times during the interview, Dorotea's small cage of para-
keets located in the kitchen would commence wildly chirping and
tweeting. In a sweet, calm voice Dorotea would say to me in
Spanish, "I hope they don't bother you too much, but you know
they are my little friends. God has given us those little animals so
that we can always have music in life."*

*Dorotea is a beautiful and sincere woman who spends her
days tending to her birds and garden. On her kitchen window sill,
she keeps a small old picture of a strange man, and next to it, a
small vase with a single flower. The story of Dorotea's simple gesture to this strange fellow in the picture now follows.*

DOROTEA RIOS'S STORY

One evening seven years ago, I was alone in my bedroom when
I heard a noise coming from the living room. I got up off my
chair and walked into the dark hallway. I turned on the light
and noticed the large figure of a man standing by the front
door. I was scared because I didn't recognize this man. I asked
him, "Who are you? What do you want?" He did not answer me,

so I said, "Please leave my house, please leave my house." Again he did not answer me. I stood there amazed that a stranger had somehow gotten into my house.

The ghost was wearing dark-colored trousers, suspenders, and a white shirt, and his hair was combed back. I also noticed that he had big ears! I began to get really frightened, and I guess he sensed this because he took some steps away from me. I let out a scream and that's when he disappeared!

Immediately I knew this was a ghost, and it left me shaking. I was so scared that night that I couldn't even think of sleeping. I decided to turn on the radio and leave all the lights on. I put on my coat and walked over to my neighbors', who lived a short walk away from me. I needed to get away from my house, I was so scared. I told my friend what I had seen, and she could see how frightened I was because I began to cry. I spent the night at her house, and in the morning she accompanied me to my house. As we entered my house—aside from the lights and radio being on—there was nothing out of place.

I had never experienced anything like this before. I began to think that I had imagined the ghost. I thought "was I going crazy?" I could not get the image of the ghost out of my mind. I guess I wanted to know who this ghost was. Was he a relative of mine, a friend, or what?

After that night, I did not experience the ghost for about a year. Then, early one morning at dawn, I was awakened by the sound of my birds making loud noises in the kitchen. As I entered the kitchen, I saw the ghost once again. This time he was seated at the table. He just stared at me with big, dark eyes. Because the kitchen windows faced East, the morning light coming through the curtains lit the room just enough for me to make out the details of his face. I got the courage to ask him to tell me who he was. He kept quiet and then slowly turned his head to one side. I saw that he had a large wet area just above his right ear. I was standing about 10 feet away, and as I stared, I noticed that he had an injury. I began to feel a weakness overcome my body. I held onto the door jam and pleaded to the ghost to leave my home.

I didn't notice when the ghost disappeared, because it happened so quickly. I phoned my neighbor, who came right over to my house. We discussed the situation, and she decided it would be best to contact a priest. I was so scared about angering the ghost that I decided not to have a priest come to the house. I didn't want to risk having this ghost return to do something to me. I just didn't want to stir things up anymore.

"She asked me if this was the ghost I had seen in my house."

My neighbor mentioned my problem to her sister who worked at the local senior center. Soon after, I received a call from a woman at the center who said that she too had heard my story and had information that I might wish to hear. I told her that I would like to visit with her, to discuss what she knew. She agreed to meet that evening at her home.

I informed my neighbor about my conversation with the woman and our meeting. I also asked if she and her sister could accompany me to this meeting. She agreed, and that night my neighbor drove the three of us to the woman's home.

The woman was surprised to see all of us, but was nonetheless, very welcoming. After I told her my story, she explained why she thought I was being visited by the ghost. The ghost, she said, was that of a man who had been a close friend of her family's. The young man's name was Edward Buckwith and he spoke fluent Spanish. He had lived in Tucson and had visited her family every time he passed through Nogales on his return trip from Mexico. He had a contact in Mexico who had supplied him with liquor. At the time, Prohibition was in full swing, and it was illegal to bring liquor into the United States. Lots of men were involved in this illegal business; it was not a safe profession.

The woman continued her story. "One evening, after having dinner at our house, Edward left our home. My parents were unaware of what happened next until the following day. Apparently, he was surrounded by some hooligans who knew he was carrying liquor, and they beat him up. One of the men kicked Edward in the head so hard, he passed out. After beating him, they rolled his body down the small ravine that used to be located next to the house. He landed face down in a small amount of water, which caused him to drown," she said.

The woman went on to say that she believed the ghost I had seen was Edward's because of my description of his large ears. Then she brought out a picture and asked me if this was the ghost I had seen in my house. I was shocked! The ghost I had seen twice in my house was now staring back at me from the picture I was holding in my hand!

The woman said, "As soon as I heard about the ears, I knew it had to be Edward." She further said, "Why Edward has chosen to appear in your house is a mystery to me." She said this because my house is not the house that her family used to live in. Her house was directly next door to my house. I didn't know how to respond, except to say that all this was making me a nervous wreck. I asked her what I could do to end his visits. She answered, "Take the picture and place it in your house and ask Eddie to go on to Heaven. Tell him you know he was murdered and that you feel sorry about this, but you can't do anything else for him."

I returned home with the picture and placed it the kitchen counter with a flower. I prayed and said the words the woman had told me to say. After a few weeks, I revisited the woman to return the picture. She asked me to keep it and display it the way I had been doing. "What good would it do me now? He chose your house, not mine."

PARKER

Parker is on the east bank of the Colorado River, 163 miles west of Phoenix. The Parker "vicinity" consists of a number of separate but interrelated areas: Parker, Parker South, the Arizona side of the Colorado river area, and the communities on the California side. Established in 1871, the town was later moved some four miles north to the site of the Atchison, Topeka, and Santa Fe Railroad crossing. At an elevation of 450 feet above sea level, Parker was founded in 1908 and incorporated in 1948. In May 1982, by initiative petition voters formed La Paz County from the northern portion of the former Yuma County. On January 1, 1983, Parker became the county seat for La Paz county.

Parker's economy is based primarily on retail trade and services. The 16-mile strip of the Colorado River, between Parker Dam and Headgate Rock Dam, forms one of the finest bodies of water in the country for water-based recreational activities. This makes Parker a major destination point for tourists and winter visitors.

∾

My interview with Brian took place at his sister-in-law's home. Brian is an 87-year-old, native-born Irishman. Born in 1910 in County Wicklow, Brian, his parents, and his two sisters arrived in the United States when he was only seven years of age. The Doran family lived in Philadelphia for 10 years, after which Brian decided to make the solo move West. His traveling eventually led him to the town of Tucson, where he worked as a construction worker. In 1968 he moved to Parker and found a job as a plumber. In 1969 he met and married Becky, a local woman originally from Colorado. The following year he and his new wife had a baby girl, whom they named Kenna. Kenna survived until age three. On the baby's death certificate, "trauma to the head due to a fall,"is listed as the cause of death.

Becky discovered little Kenna's lifeless body on the kitchen floor one afternoon. Kenna had apparently run into the table, hit her head, and knocked herself unconscious. Becky was hanging the wet laundry in the backyard and did not notice what had happened. She went to check on her baby whom she had laid on the living room sofa for a noon-time nap just an hour or so before.

After the death of their daughter, the Dorans did not have any more children. In 1975 Becky herself was involved in a car accident on Interstate 10 and died.

There's no doubt that Brian has suffered many deep heartaches in his life. Given his trials, he remains focused on celebrating life and told to me his personal dictum on life: "God put us here on earth to be judged, not to judge."

There remains much to be told of Brian's life; What follows is only one segment of that fascinating and at times difficult unwritten biography of this special man.

BRIAN DORAN'S STORY

The death of my little girl left both my wife and I with an empty hole in our lives. We had been so happy; Kenna had brought us so much joy and pride. My wife and I were never fully convinced about what caused our baby's death. How could a fall have caused a three-year-old's death? The doctor who examined Kenna's body told us that because she hit her head with such force, it had caused a bruise or blood clot to form on her brain. This blood clot affected her lungs, and she stopped breathing. With no oxygen reaching her brain, the brain became damaged, and she died.

With the death of our little Kenna, our dreams ended. Soon my wife's personality changed. Becky no longer laughed. We began to argue, and our marriage was in trouble. We were filled with depression and sadness. Not long after, my wife was taken away from me in a car accident.

So now I was left totally alone in an empty house. I was such an emotional mess during that time. I was fortunate to have the members of my church, who helped me through the tough times. They also helped with Becky's funeral arrangements. When the time came to pack and donate my wife's clothes and my daughter's toys and things—well, if not for their help, I don't know what I would have done. It was just a few weeks later that I was visited by my baby's spirit.

I was sitting in the living room one evening listening to a radio talk show. It was about 9:30 p.m. All the lights in the house were out except for the light over the stove and a lamp on my livingroom table. Suddenly, I heard the sound of a coughing child. I turned to look in the direction of the kitchen and I saw, standing in the doorway, my little girl! I was so shocked to see her that I could not move. Instead of immediately saying something, I began to sob like a baby!

It took me a few seconds, but soon I called out her name. I felt her unblinking eyes stare deep into my soul. "Kenna, my little Kenna," I cried, "I've missed you so much!" She responded to my plea by raising her arms and placing her hands to her throat. This gesture told me something was wrong. Quietly, and with much pain on her little face, she began to cough and rub her throat once again. Try as I might, I could not get up off the chair. It was as if I were glued firmly in place!

I cried out, "Baby, what is wrong with your throat?" Again

she rubbed her neck and made sounds of painful suffering. I said, "What is wrong with your throat? What is it?"

Then she cried out, "Daddy, Daddy!" At that point I was overwhelmed with a deep feeling of despair and helplessness. I broke down into an uncontrollable, shaking, and crying mess. I wanted to help and go to my child, but I could not move out of the chair! I sobbed and sobbed and when I looked up at her, she again said, "Daddy!"

I answered, "Yes, yes, baby, I know you hurt! I promise I will help you!" Then she slowly disappeared! I soon regained the ability to lift myself out of the chair, went to my bedroom, and cried myself to sleep. I knew that Kenna had appeared to me for a reason. The following day an answer came to me.

The next morning, I was in the backyard mending a wire fence. Strangely, I heard a voice in my head, telling me to contact the local cemetery office. I had always had doubts about my daughter's cause of death. I was never fully satisfied with the doctor's summary.

Now the apparition of my daughter the night before had only caused me to wonder even more. I needed to know once and for all how she died. If it would take another autopsy, well, so be it! I could not erase the image of Kenna's little spirit coughing and rubbing her throat from my mind.

I contacted the cemetery office and also spoke to our local marshall about the possibility of an autopsy. I was met with strange looks, but overall, everything went smoothly. They informed me that there was no reason why I could not go through with my desire, but I would have to contact a medical examiner in Phoenix, to do the actual autopsy. Of course, I did not tell the marshall about my daughter's ghostly visit, or anything else which might give anyone cause to view me as a crazy old man. It took a few weeks to get the necessary paperwork, and within a couple of months, everything was in place.

The total cost for an autopsy was unbelievably expensive, but I was determined. The memory of Kenna standing in the kitchen doorway with such a painful expression on her face gave me the strength I needed to push ahead. Finally, the day of the disinterment took place, and my little girl's body and coffin were taken to a medical lab in Phoenix.

Tissue, hair, and blood samples were taken, as were x-rays. After 20 days, I received a phone call from the lab and was asked to drive to Phoenix. The attending doctor wanted to speak with me in person. I arrived at the lab and was escorted into a room with a light box on the wall, used for viewing x-rays. Soon the doctor and a medical assistant, carrying an oversize envelope of x-rays, entered the room.

The doctor informed me of the tests results. She stated that all the tests showed Kenna to be in normal health at the time of her death. I was relieved to hear this, but before I could feel content with this updated information, the doctor switched on the light box and removed from the envelope the x-rays taken of Kenna's small head and neck. Immediately, I knew that something was not right. On the x-rays was a small object that showed up as a bright white little square in Kenna's throat!

The doctor told me that when she had viewed the x-rays,

it was clear that this unusual square object needed to be investigated. When the foreign object was removed from Kenna's little throat, the doctor discovered that it was a sewing thimble! The doctor estimated that Kenna must have swallowed the thimble, and it had lodged in her throat, causing her to choke. In a panic, Kenna must have run throughout the house, reached the kitchen, lost consciousness, fainted, and hit her head. The trauma to her head was obvious because of the skin bruising and the large swollen area where she hit the table. This visible sign of injury was enough for the initial examiner to conclude his reason for her cause of death.

I was both greatly surprised and immediately satisfied with the results of this second autopsy. A feeling of satisfaction came over me. No longer did I have any doubts; no longer did the cause of my one and only child's death haunt me. Finally the spirit of my baby girl would be at peace.

On the return drive home to Parker from Phoenix, I could only imagine what my wife's reaction might have been if she were still alive. I believe that Kenna's ghostly visitation was for a purpose. She wanted me to be at peace, to know that her Daddy would also find peace from his loneliness. No one can ever tell me that there is no life after death. I have seen my baby, and I know better!

PHOENIX

Phoenix, known as the Valley of the Sun, is the seventh largest city in the nation. The city is the hub of the rapidly growing Southwest. Phoenix also is the capital of Arizona and the Maricopa County seat. In 1867, Phoenix founder Jack Swilling formed a canal company and diverted irrigation water from the Salt River. Soon many farms were operating, but drought periods hampered production. In 1911, Roosevelt Dam was completed and water supplies were stabilized. Cotton and citrus became the most important crops.

Phoenix's explosive growth began during World War II when military airfields were built in Maricopa County for the near-perfect flying weather. Many defense industries followed. Luke Air Force Base, west of Phoenix, is still a major training center for fighter pilots.

The Phoenix climate has been a major factor in its economic development: the area experiences sunshine nearly every day of the year.

The name Phoenix—the legendary Egyptian symbol of rebirth—was chosen because the city was built on the ruins of the Hohokam Indian civilization, whose farmers laid out irrigation canals still in use today.

Phoenix has a diversified economic base. Manufacturing is a leading employer with 148,000 people working for 3,100 firms in the metro area. Electronics is a strong component. The area currently ranks third among electronic production centers in the country. Tourism is an important income producer. Many world-class hotels and resorts cater to visitors.

∼

I interviewed Yolanda at her home on the far north side of the city. Yolanda has lived in Phoenix for 14 years. Born and raised in Phoenix, she moved to Los Angeles to attend college and eventually marry. Her marriage was in her own words, "a disaster." After her divorce, single and without children, this 42-year-old woman decided to return to the city of her birth. She bought a small lot of land on the north side of the city, and purchased a two-bedroom mobile home.

Due to the extreme heat that Phoenix is famous for, Yolanda built a ramada (arbor) directly outside her front door, and under which our interview was conducted. While sitting under its protective wood slats, the ramada offered us much-welcomed shade from the intense heat of the day. Looking out from the ramada to the north is a dramatic, panoramic view of the Tonto National Forest. This forest is composed of a blanket of desert flora, including saguaro cactus, paloverde (green thin-trunked trees), prickly pear, and other such drought tolerant plants. The mountains rise in their unique and contorted splendor up to the blue sky. What a sight! "I love it here," Yolanda said, "I have several coyotes come visit me each night. They sniff around and catch any mice that might want to make a dash inside my home."

Looking to the east, my eyes caught the sight of several large homes, and further beyond, even more indications of human encroachment upon the desert landscape. "Things sure have changed here since I was a child," Yolanda said "My whole family used to hike in the foothills each summer and gather saguaro tunas (fruit). Mom would make a jam out of the tunas. It was delicious! Now with all the changes and rapid growth of this city, it's hard for me to even comprehend how things used to be back then."

I had a wonderful time listening to Yolanda's stories about the times she spent up in the mountains. I especially enjoyed the story she told me about the time she and a girlfriend hiked into the Tontos one spring and experienced something unforgettable— something frighteningly unforgettable.

YOLANDA HUERTA'S STORY

Last year my friend Erlinda and I were sitting right out here one evening, under this ramada. We were enjoying a few beers and talking about how frustrated we both were about how life was going for us. We decided that the best thing for us to do would be to get away from "the world" and hike for a couple of days and nights into the mountains. We had done this before, so we were well prepared for the journey. Our sleeping bags and backpacks were dusted off, and within two days we were off!

The first day of our journey was wonderful. We had brought along plenty of water and food so we knew we would get along fine. On our second day, we decided to change our usual course, which was to follow the trail north, veering to the east, hoping to go around a large mountain and meet up with the trail up ahead. We hiked for hours, until the sun began to cast long shadows on the ground. Earlier in the day, we had decided to make camp for the night while the sun was still out. We spotted a blue tent just off the trail about a mile ahead. As we got closer, we heard beautiful music. A small dog barked at us as we approached the tent, and a young guy who was playing a flute turned and waved hello to us. We stopped and talked to this interesting guy. He was from Taos, New Mexico. After a while, we were

"... she ran into a small grove of paloverdes."

introduced to his wife, who we had awakened from her nap in the tent. They invited us to pitch our tent next to theirs for the night. Erlinda and I agreed that it would be a good idea, so we chose a patch of ground with the least amount of rocks and pitched our tent.

We had an interesting conversation with our new friends about city life versus living with just the basics as we passed around a bag of trail mix. Even though the sun was just setting in the West, there was still plenty of light. Suddenly, their dog began to growl at something in the distance. We stopped our conversation to look and see what the dog was barking at. We were surprised to see the figure of a woman running over the landscape, about a 200 feet from us. She was a short woman and had shoulder length hair. Surprisingly, she was naked and holding on to her stomach! We were definitely caught off guard by the woman. I yelled at her, and she must have heard me, because she stopped running and turned to faced us. We could see that she was not acting in a normal manner. Again I yelled, and she just stood there, frozen in place. Erlinda said she was going to walk over to the woman. I decided to go as well.

As we came to about 40 or 50 feet from her, she turned away and ran into a small grove of paloverdes. We got close enough to her to see her facial features. The woman was an American Indian. What instantly alarmed us was the *blood* that covered her hands and stomach! I yelled at her not to run away, as both Erlinda and I attempted to catch up to her. When we got to the paloverdes, there was no trace of her. She had disappeared! There was no way anyone could have gotten away from us that quickly. The whole episode left us disturbed. The poor woman's face was filled with so much fear and panic. It was difficult to get that picture out of my mind. Just then, the couple we were camping with came up to us.

The wife asked us where the woman went. We had no answer. They must have seen the look of amazement on our faces because they lowered their voices and said, "Are you all right? What happened, what did you see?" I began to shake with fear as I answered, "We've just seen a ghost!" Erlinda said, "Let's get the hell out of here, *now!*" Once back at the camp we told them the details of the woman and her bloody stomach.

The couple decided, while there was still enough light, to return to the grove of paloverdes and search for the woman. They looked everywhere in the general area. The couple's dog sniffed the ground but did not seem to pick up any scent. After a while searching, they decided to stop since it was getting dark, and they didn't want to risk the chance of getting bitten by a rattlesnake.

That night it took Erlinda and me a very long time before we felt comfortable enough to fall asleep. The couple who also saw the woman from a distance must have had many more questions they wanted to ask us, but under the circumstances they must have sensed that it would be best to save their questions for the morning.

Morning finally did arrive—not soon enough for Erlinda and me. We discussed the details of the night before and returned to the site of the woman's disappearance. Once again, we did not find a clue or any indication of what had transpired the evening before. Erlinda turned to me and said, "I think it would be best if we hiked back home today, what do yout think?"

I didn't need any further prodding. I answered, "Let's get going!" We said our goodbyes to the couple from Taos and headed on the trail back home.

As you can imagine, all Erlinda and I talked about was the woman. We tried to make sense of what we had seen, but it only caused us to have more questions about something that seemed impossible to explain.

Once at home, I bought and read our local newspapers for any report of a woman who had disappeared or been reported missing. I didn't find a thing. The local television news didn't report any missing woman either. Erlinda and I decided to drop the subject and get on with our lives. However, my curiosity prompted me to pick up the phone and give my uncle a call. My uncle is retired after working 25 years for the forest service as a surveyor. I decided to give him a call simply to inquire about anything unusual that he may have experienced or heard of during his employment. He found my questions to be rather odd, but soon told me about several fellow workers who had encountered a woman's ghost that fit my description.

He told me that about 10 years ago, two men were surveying a small track of land further north of the area where Erlinda and I had seen the ghost. He said that the men saw this strange Indian woman running naked among some short desert brush. Aside from her nakedness, the men were interested in another odd occurrence. Getting a better view with binoculars, they could see her disappear and reappear! All this took place in broad daylight.

The woman appeared sporadically and watched the men at their work for the full four days that they were in the area. She never got any closer than several hundred yards from where they were. It was obvious to them that she did not want anyone approaching her. Not wanting to arouse any jokes from their fellow workers back at the office, the two men kept the ghost woman a secret from the other employees. My uncle was the only friend whom they had felt secure enough to trust with their information. Aside from what my uncle knew from rumors, he was unaware of anyone else experiencing any strange apparitions of this ghostly Native American woman.

Erlinda and I have not heard any more about this ghost. I would like to know what she is doing up there in the desert among the cactus and boulders. Does she have something to tell us about how she died? Who killed her perhaps? Maybe she has appeared to someone else. Whatever the story, I won't be hiking in that part of the mountains ever again.

TOMBSTONE

Tombstone, In Cochise County, is probably the most famous and most glamorized mining town in America. Prospector Ed Schieffeling was told he would only find his tombstone in the "Apache-infested" San Pedro Valley. Thus he named his first silver claim Tombstone, and it became the name of the town. On a mesa between the Dragoon and Huachuca Mountains at an elevation of 4,540 feet, Tombstone was incorporated in 1881.

While the area later became notorious for saloons, gambling houses, and the Earp-Clanton shoot-out, in the 1880s Tombstone was larger than Tucson and had become the most cultivated city in the West. Massive underground water in the mines and falling silver prices ended the boom in 1886. Having survived the Great Depression and removal of the County Seat to Bisbee, Tombstone in the 1930s became known as the "Town Too Tough To Die."

Tombstone's economy has changed drastically since its days as a mining town. The town's colorful history is the key factor in its steady growth. In 1962, the Department of the Interior designated Tombstone a Registered Historical Landmark. A restoration zone was established and a commission organized for the preservation of its landmarks. Tourists flock to the town by the thousands, and their business is the mainstay of the economy.

BIG NOSE KATE'S SALOON

In the 1800's, "Big Nose Kate's Saloon" was once The Grand Hotel. Although the saloon itself was not in existence during Tombstone's rise to fame, it has on its own made quite a mark on Tombstone. The saloon is named after the woman who had quite a rambunctious relationship with John Henry "Doc" Holliday. Doc, a former dentist and a well known gambler in town, never married Kate, although she remained his live-in girlfriend for many years. This great hotel hosted such infamous personalities as Wyatt and Virgil Earp, Holliday, the Clantons, and the McLaurys.

Debbie K. Valdez, Teresa Rice,
Tim and Macy Ferrick

The bar of the present saloon is located on the first floor, but originally, when it was The Grand Hotel, the bar was located downstairs in the basement. The present bar is the only Tombstone bar that is still in use to this very day.

THE LEGEND OF "THE SWAMPER"

During the The Grand Hotel's golden era, a man known as "The Swamper" who worked as a janitor also did odd jobs for the hotel in exchange for his room and board. He was a trusted and honest hotel aid. The Swamper had his own special bedroom, located in the dark basement of the hotel, which he used as his own private haven. He enjoyed the peace and solitude where, separated from the hustle and bustle of the hotel's many guests above, he could keep his secret of his silvery wealth to himself.

Throughout the years The Swamper had hoarded and concealed a small fortune of silver somewhere on the premises of The Grand Hotel. The basement where he lived was deep enough below the surface of the ground to afford entrance into one of the catacombing mine shafts that ran underground, beneath the hotel as well as beneath most of Tombstone. The Swamper spent many painstaking hours over a period of years tunneling an entrance into this silver mine shaft. Completing his task, he gained access to a thick vein of silver where he secretly extracted, ounce by ounce, glorious silver nuggets.

To this day it is unknown whether The Swamper spent his silver before his death or hoarded it in an unknown niche somewhere on the premises of the hotel. Employees of Big Nose Kate's Saloon however, swear that they have seen The Swamper's ghost wandering the halls and stairs. Photographers have caught the ghostly image of an unknown being on a photo as well as on the postcard of the saloon's interior. Perhaps the The Swamper, in his afterlife, is protecting the silver still buried somewhere in this legendary building.

I interviewed the following employees of the present Big Nose Kate's Saloon on a very hot midday in July. I was thoroughly amazed by everyone's serene composure and easygoing manner as they described their stories.

At one point during the interviews, I was led down a narrow wooden staircase to the basement of the saloon where the owner, Mr. Steve Goldstein, pointed out the actual silver mine shaft from which many stories evolved, including the one of The Swamper. For safety's sake, the mine shaft can now be seen through bars of iron. Arranged around the shaft's opening is a collection of antique period furniture of the 1800s. This strange accumulation of dusty furniture, picks, shovels, mirrors, clothing, and oil lamps is made visible only by a few spooky-colored lightbulbs, which cast an eerie glow on what a miner's life might have looked like.

The stories of the ghosts of Tombstone's violent past will continually resurface. I now present to you just a few of the testimonies from some living individuals who have been witness to weird happenings at Big Nose Kate's Saloon.

TIM L. FERRICK'S STORY

I am currently the manager of the saloon and have held this position for nine months. I'm originally from Southern California and have visited Arizona and Tombstone repeatedly throughout the last four years. During one of my visits to Tombstone, I visited my brother Mick, who at the time was the manager of the saloon. He has since died and is buried at the local cemetery. Before my brother died, he mentioned to me that he himself had experienced "ghosts" at the saloon. About one month after his funeral, I made plans with my wife to return to Tombstone and meet with the owner of the saloon about taking over my brother's job.

We arrived at Tombstone in the late evening. The owner had closed the doors for the night, and we sat at a table at one corner of the saloon drinking sodas. We discussed a few personal issues, and for some reason, the conversation turned to the strange, ghostly things that employees have experienced at the saloon. Approximately, half an hour into our discussion, a sudden movement caught all our eyes.

We all turned to look up in the direction of the ceiling of the saloon where a small balcony is located. On the balcony were two mannequins, a man and a woman dressed in 1800s period clothing. We watched as the female mannequin, seated far behind the railing, moved to the railing of the balcony, leaned over, and fell to the floor! As we all sat in our chairs stunned by the noise of the mannequin making contact with the floor, I spotted the male mannequin, who was left facing us. I said to the others at the table, "Hey, take a look at the other mannequin." We all watched as the male mannequin's head quickly turned towards the direction where the female mannequin had been! Truly unnerved by this, we promptly got out of our chairs and called it a night.

The next morning, when I spoke to the manager, she stated that she had no explanation for what had happened. She considered it to be her first ghostly experience at the saloon.

My second experience at the saloon took place about one month after I had begun working there. It was about 7:30 a.m. when I began to hear doors opening and closing on their own. I walked to the now opened door—which I had closed and locked just minutes before from the inside—only to see it in an open position! Lights that I personally had turned off were now turned on. During these times, I was the only one in the building!

Returning to my office chair, I suddenly began to hear noises coming from down in the basement where the mine shaft is located. These were the distinctive sounds that a man wearing heavy boots with spurs would make as he walked up or down the stairs. The sound was that of someone only walking half way up, or down, the stairs, and stopping in the middle.

A few times, after hearing the steps, I rushed to the stairs, hoping to catch a sight of the person making the noise. But as soon as I reached the stairs, the footsteps would abruptly stop!

Sometime after these incidents, we decided to install surveillance cameras throughout the saloon. We spent several days installing the cameras in just the right locations, in key rooms of the saloon. The equipment functioned with motion detectors that would sense movement and automatically turn the cameras on to record whatever was present. These sensors were very sensitive to movement, and I was sure we would be able to record any burglar ghost on film. That night before we left the saloon, I personally turned on the motion detectors.

The next morning as I unlocked the back door and entered the building, my wife and I were surprised to see that all the cupboards, doors, refrigerator doors, and drawers were wide open! Nothing had been stolen from the premises. The alarm had not been activated, and I immediately phoned the alarm company to complain that their equipment had failed. The alarm company sent representatives who came over, tested the system, and found that everything was functioning correctly.

Another experience both my wife and I had took place one morning. I switched the monitors that were attached to the cameras to scan each room. The camera that was placed in the dance floor of the saloon was picking up a noise. I called my wife over to the TV monitor, and as I turned up the volume, we both clearly heard the sound of booted footsteps walking across the floor! We immediately left the office and entered the dance room where we discovered nothing out of place. A few minutes later, we heard the same footsteps walking in the opposite direction. We knew that something ghostly was happening, but just decided to live with it.

Throughout the years, we have had many patrons experience odd things. Just recently, I was called to witness a gentleman who was in the downstairs bar going through his own supernatural experience. I witnessed the jacket he was wearing being pressed flat against his body! It was as if a large pane of glass was being pressed against him. His wife took a picture of her husband as he was going through the experience, and when she developed it, the large image of a butcher knife appeared floating next to his head! I must admit this incident left me with goose bumps.

Other things that have taken place—strangely enough to just our female employees—have been trash can lids rising off the cans and dropping to the floor, rolling large circular patterns on the floor of the basement. This has happened several times to my own wife. My wife now refers to the ghost as "Felix." It's just a name she decided upon, to give the ghost a personality. The male employees have not experienced such things, only the women. We have since removed the trash cans from the basement.

The current owner, Gloria Goldstein, and I heard Gloria's name being called out in a very loud, distinctive male voice. We both turned around as she responded, "Yes." There was no answer.

Other events patrons have experienced have been the sound of gambling dice being dropped to the floor, sudden cold winds, severe pressure changes in rooms, etc. A lot of these incidents take place randomly. We never gave thought to contacting a priest. We knew we had a ghost and that was it. I know that there is the presence of someone still here in the building. Perhaps a ghost is protecting the place. I'm not afraid, but I do let our employees feel comfortable enough to approach me with their concerns.

MARCY D. FERRICK'S STORY

My husband Tim and I began employment at the saloon at the same time. I was present in the saloon the evening that Tim has spoken about, when we had our first experience with the mannequins coming to life. I gotta say that what we experienced, that night with those mannequins, was enough to send us out of there fast!

My second experience with "Felix" happened when I was in the basement. As I entered the basement, suddenly the lid on the trash can popped off and began to roll on the floor. The lid made small circular movements, and then they got bigger and bigger. It just kept moving until I took hold of it and placed it back on the can. Then once more it popped off and repeated the same circular motions on the floor. Again, I took hold of the lid and placed it on the can. Well, this happened for about five times until I had had enough. In a loud and irritated voice I said, "Stop it now!" Then it stopped. I think that "Felix" is trying to harass or tease the women. I don't get the feeling that he wants to hurt us, just to let us know that he is still here.

Just a couple of months ago, we had two patrons who were very drunk disturbing other patrons with their loud voices. I decided to ask them to leave. When I approached the table, I immediately felt the strong pressure of an invisible male hand on my shoulder. Before I had even said a word, the two drunks gazed with very wide eyes in the direction past my shoulder, and immediately put their beers on the table, got up, and made for the door! I then felt the pressure on my shoulder slowly lift up and disappear.

Another strange thing that happens is when I walk down the stairs to the basement. Sometimes I'll notice that the ceiling fan is turning. Thinking that it has been left on, I'll reach for the electrical switch and notice that it is in the "off" position! I'm at a loss to find an explanation for this. We have had the switches checked and have found nothing wrong with the electrical system.

Given all that the other employees and I have experienced in the saloon, I am convinced that it is haunted! I still hear the very distinct footsteps of a heavy-booted and spurred man, who walks up and down the stairs that lead to the basement. I think that the reason "Felix" is so active in the saloon is because he is trapped between the world of the living and of the dead. The first experience I had with the mannequins shocked me and, yes, I was scared, but all the other experiences since have just become a nuisance to me. I'm not scared to be in the building by myself, but you never know what "he" might decide to do next time.

THERESA RICE'S STORY

I'm originally from Tyler, Texas, and have been working at the saloon for seven months as a waitress. My first experience with the ghost of the saloon happened only two weeks after I started work. It was around high noon when I was standing on the south end of the bar.

I was talking to a gentleman customer who was seated across the bar from me. Suddenly, I felt the presence of someone behind me and just as quickly, felt two fingers give my rear end two hard pinches! I immediately turned around to confront the vulgar man who had rudely done this, but when I turned there was no one there! I had been told by other employees that the saloon was haunted. After this experience, I was definitely convinced of this.

My second experience happened just about two months ago. Again, this took place at about noon. I was walking toward the bar, carrying a tray of drinks. Suddenly, I heard a loud male voice call out, "Theresa!" I turned and saw no one. This has happened more than once to me, and also in the presence of others. This initially left me with a confused feeling, but soon I realized that Felix was behind it. "Felix" is the name the employees have given to what we believe to be "The Swamper." Anyway, I knew Felix was behind everything. I don't know why he chose to play these rude-natured pranks on me. Why is he trying to provoke me? I just wish he would just come out and speak to me. I don't think I would be frightened, but maybe I might be.

DEBBIE K. VALDEZ'S STORY

I'm originally from Whiteland, Indiana, and have been working as a bartender in the second bar that's located downstairs in the basement. I also have a country music band, "Black Velvet," that performs at the saloon. So I'm both a bartender and entertainer. I've been employed at Big Nose Kate's now for seven months. My first experience took place five months after I had begun working at the saloon.

It was in the early afternoon when I happened to look up to where the mannequins were located on the balcony. I spotted a very nicely dressed woman whom I had never seen before. She was dressed in the style of the 1800s—dark dress, holding a parasol, and her hair was done up in ringlets that were shoulder length. I could not keep my eyes off this strangely beautiful woman. As much as I stared at her, she did not look in my direction, but appeared happy to just observe everyone else down below. Soon I became frightened and felt a coldness come over me. Eventually she disappeared, and I have not seen her since.

Another time, I was wearing my hair pulled back and held in place with a large white bow. Well, apparently the ghost "Felix" wanted to play with my bow because he kept pulling on it. Several times, I turned my head to see who was tugging at my hair and bow. There was not a living soul. Well, after a few hours of this I got tired of his game and I said, "Now, you stop it!" After that he left me alone.

The ghost also hides my pens. I will write a guest receipt and place the pen on the cash register as I hand the receipt to the customer. I won't even leave the register. As I reach for my pen—*poof*—it's gone! This has happened when more than one person is with me. We look on the floor, behind the register, everywhere! Then in a few minutes, the pen reappears right where I had originally placed it! Now, is that weird or what?

"I'm not scared, just a little nervous to be down there."

I tend to see lights go on and off in rooms when no one else is with me. I see this quite a lot. I also have seen a gentleman who will sit at the basement bar, wearing a long-sleeved white shirt. He just appears quite suddenly, and then just as quickly will disappear. I get the feeling that the ghost does not want to cause me harm, but I have to admit I get very cold chills when I experience these things. The ghost is a playful spirit, and knowing this, I don't like to be left alone in the basement bar. If we have no patrons down below, I'll just walk upstairs to be with someone. I'm not scared, just a little nervous to be alone down there.

Tucson

Tucson, nicknamed "The Old Pueblo," is Arizona's oldest city, with a unique blend of Native American, Spanish, Mexican, and Anglo heritages. The second largest city in the state, Tucson is modern, with high tech industries and world-class cultural events, yet it retains the charm of its desert frontier roots.

Tucson is a Native American word that translates as "water at black mountain." Located beside the Santa Cruz River, it has been home to Native American villages and farms for at least 2,000 years. In 1700, Father Kino established the first Spanish mission, San Xavier, at the Native American village of Bac, 10 miles south of Tucson.

Tucson was founded in 1775 as a Spanish (presidio) or military garrison to protect settlers from Apache raids. It was governed by Mexico from 1821 until 1854, when the Gadsden Purchase made it a part of the United States. Tucson was once the territorial capital of Arizona.

Tucson was incorporated in 1877 and is the Pima County seat. At 2,389 feet, it is known for its mild winters and very hot summers.

~

My interview with Florencio was conducted entirely in Spanish, in the same house the Saenz family has owned for over 70 years. Florencio lived in the family's house with his wife of 41 years until her death 12 years ago. They had no children, and today Florencio lives alone in the house with his cat, Pepino.

Aside from the following story of his uncle, Florencio provided me with numerous details about his life in Tucson. His detailed description of Chicano family life and the various hardships experienced along the way were at times quite touching to hear.

"All us families—the Saenzses, Ortegas, Valenzuelas, Rioses, Barrelas—would gather and have big get-togethers at each other's houses. Those were real nice times. We were all good friends. Some of our children grew up and even married into each other's families. Now, all the old ones from that time are either dead or have moved away."

Today, Florencio spends his days gardening, reading, and attending local church functions. On his bedroom dresser sits a plain old shoe box. Inside is a folded, white cotton cloth containing what remains of four red carnations. "My family has kept these remains for many, many years. I'll always remember the day they arrived in our living room."

FLORENCIO SAENZ'S STORY

I have lived in Tucson all my life. My grandparents were originally from Mesilla, New Mexico, and after they married in the 1920s, they moved to Tucson. We were a very close-knit family, and I was especially close to my father's younger brother, my uncle Julian. As a child, I followed my uncle Julian everywhere. Our family pictures always showed the two of us together. We were inseparable!

Sadly, as my uncle was driving to work one day, he was involved in a serious auto accident. The driver of the other car died at the scene. My uncle was taken to the hospital and placed in the intensive care unit. He was not expected to live for very long.

I took the news very hard, and I remember visiting the hospital with my family and viewing his nearly lifeless body. The awful memories that I can't erase are viewing him in the bed, hooked up to all the tubes, the smell of the room, and the whole atmosphere of the hospital room. It was a terrible time for me. My uncle survived for two weeks in this condition and never regained consciousness.

Late one night, my mother received the phone call that informed us of my uncle's passing. I remember hearing the phone ring and immediately knew that it had to be about my uncle. I was a young boy of 14 years, and his death left a strong impression on me. I refused to eat for several days and would not speak with anyone. I stayed in my room and even refused to watch my favorite television shows. I became so overcome with sadness that my parents had our local priest come to our home to speak with me. The conversation with the priest did me good, and in a few days, I came out of my depressed state.

My father had a nice picture of my uncle in a drawer with other family pictures. He and my mother decided to frame the picture and display it in our living room. The picture was placed on top of a coffee table together with a small burning candle. It was about a month or so after Uncle Julian was laid to rest that a strange thing began to happen to me.

One evening, as my family and I were gathered in the living room watching television, I turned my head and looked in the direction where my father was seated. There, standing directly behind my father, was Uncle Julian! I was stunned and unable to speak. I could clearly see my uncle as he looked at me and smiled. He held onto the back of my father's chair. Somehow I knew that I was to keep quiet and not alarm my family. My uncle was speaking to me without moving his mouth. I nervously smiled back and soon the tears began to surface in my eyes. I heard my sister say, "Mom, look at Florencio. He's crying!" As I heard my mother ask me what's wrong, the image of my uncle slowly disappeared.

I got up from my chair and ran to my bedroom. I cried and my mother ran to me. As my mother held me in her arms, I told her what I had just seen. The rest of my family gathered in my bedroom to hear my story. My father put his hands to his face and cried out, "Julian, Julian. God bless you, my brother!"

The second time that my uncle appeared to me took place in the kitchen as we were all having dinner. Again, I saw him standing, but this time he was not behind my father; he stood in the doorway that led from the kitchen to the living room. I didn't cry. This time I just watched in amazement. He gave me a big smile, and I even saw his teeth. I calmly stated to everyone, "My uncle is standing over there; do you see him?" Everyone got quiet and turned in the direction of the doorway. I said, "Look, he's right there!"

"Are you sure?" they responded.

I answered, "Oh, yes, he's right there looking at us." I guess my uncle decided that he had given us enough of a sign because soon his image disappeared.

Throughout the weeks that followed, I saw my uncle appear to me three more times. I decided to keep his appearances to myself, for fear that I might upset my parents. Every time that my uncle appeared, he did not speak to me. His usual posture was to stand at a distance from me and smile. After the the last time he appeared to me, I decided to speak to our family priest about this. I was instructed by the priest to pray and ask my uncle's spirit to go to heaven and be at peace. I did as I was instructed, and I did not see my uncle's spirit for a long time after.

One Saturday, my parents decided to take the family to my uncle's graveside and place red carnations—Julian's favorite flowers—at his grave. As I remember, it was a cold but clear day. As we all took turns placing a carnation on the grave, my father broke down with emotion and sobbed. My mother held his hand and tried to console him. Suddenly, I saw the spirit of my uncle appear once again to me. This time there was a difference in his image. He appeared to be more "misty" and he actually spoke!

He said, "Don't be sad. I'm doing very well, and I'm very happy now." As soon as he said these words, his image faded. I told my father what I had just seen and heard.

My father responded, "Florencio, please don't tell me about your dreams anymore. Please, I'm not interested in them!" I knew that I had upset my father and so I kept quiet. We left the cemetery and ate lunch at a local restaurant. My father must have felt that he had hurt my feelings with his words. He told me that sometimes imagination plays tricks on the eyes, and perhaps I should think about what I had been seeing as being something that my imagination conjured up. I knew that what I had seen was my uncle, but not wanting to upset my father any more, I agreed with him and kept quiet.

When we arrived home, a neighbor met us in our front yard and engaged both my parents in conversation. After a few minutes, my mother excused herself and opened the front door to our house and walked inside. She called out to my father who was still speaking with the neighbor to come inside the house. As my father and my sister and I entered the living room, on the coffee table we spotted next to my uncle's picture four red carnations!

My mother was shaking with emotion as she said, "Who put these flowers here?" There were no visitors that the neighbor informed us of. My father picked up the flowers, and as he held them he said, "It doesn't matter. It's a sign from my brother that he is now doing fine." I knew then that my uncle Julian had given my family a sign to convince them of his appearances

I spoke up and said, "Yes, my uncle is going to be fine. I told you he spoke to me. Everything is going to be fine."

And so it has been.

WICKENBURG

Wickenburg is 50 miles northwest of Phoenix at an elevation of 2,100 feet. Nestled in the foothills of the Bradshaw Mountains, and along the banks of the Hassayampa River, Wickenburg boasts a rich Western history, still evident today. The town is the oldest north of Tucson.

In 1863, Henry Wickenburg discovered the Vulture Mine, which in time became the richest gold mine in Arizona's history. In the early 1900s, as the mine played out, ranching and tourism took over as the economic mainstay of the area. Wickenburg was incorporated in 1909.

Today, Wickenburg offers a relaxing western lifestyle, with a full range of municipal and private sector services.

Traditionally, tourism, cattle ranching, and agriculture have been the main economic activities in Wickenburg. There has also been a small amount of gold mining still in the area. In 1964, Wickenburg began to diversify its economic base by developing an industrial airpark to encourage manufacturing firms to locate to the town.

~

The interview with Judy took place at her home. Judy is a 58-year-old widow. She has lived in Wickenburg for 31 years. Originally she and her husband, Raphael, lived in the southernmost area of the state, in the town of Nogales. There they owned a small furniture business importing furniture from old Mexico. Judy sold their business in 1965 after Raphael suffered a fatal heart attack. Left with a young son to raise, she decided to use her keen business sense, she decided to relocate to central Arizona to the town of Wickenburg and open a Mexican restaurant.

Judy bought her current home in 1966. Judy chose not to remarry. Her only son, who visits her regularly, now lives close by. Judy's experience with ghostly hauntings have all taken place in her home and have indeed given her some very frightful moments. Her story that follows will offer some eerie proof of the existence of life after death.

JUDY LUNA'S STORY

There are so many things I can tell you about this house and my experiences, I just don't know where to begin. Both my son and I have seen the ghost of a woman appear to us during the day and night. Even a few neighbors and visitors to our house have seen the ghost's telltale signs. You can bet these experiences left them scared out of their wits! I guess the best place to start my story is when we moved into the house.

When I bought the house 31 years ago, it was in need of many repairs. Even though I knew I would have to invest quite a bit of money to do the necessary repairs, I fell in love with the house as soon as I laid eyes on it. Without the support of my friends and family, who drove from Nogales to help, it would have been impossible for me to make the move.

My brother and father helped with the major repairs on the house, and when they felt I was able to tackle the remainder of the minor fix-ups, they returned to Nogales. My neighbors were very helpful throughout my first year, offering their advice on which local plumbers and electricians to use. They recommended a very wonderful man (who was originally from Mexico) living in Wickenburg. He was an expert in building and repairing stone walls. I knew I had made a good decision to move to Wickenburg. However, it was not long before strange things began to happen in the house that caused me to question this decision.

The first ghostly incident took place one evening in the kitchen. My son and I were sitting at the table finishing our dinner. At the time of this incident, I was a smoker. I got the urge to smoke a cigarette, so I reached for my purse.

I pulled a cigarette out of the pack, got up out of my chair, and walked to the pantry where I kept the box of matchsticks. Placing the cigarette in my mouth, I turned the matchbox on its side and carefully took hold of the match. I dragged it against the striking surface of the box. There was a spark as the match was lit. As I raised the lit match to my cigarette, suddenly the lit match left my fingers and sailed across the kitchen! It hovered above the kitchen table for about five seconds before coming down and landing between my son's legs!

It all happened very fast, and I was left with my mouth wide open. My son yelled with pain as the match burned his leg. I quickly came to my senses and rushed to him. Thankfully, he was not badly burned, but was startled nonetheless. I knew that this was not something normal. I had no explanation for how this could have happened without someone or something ghostly being involved.

After this, strange things began to happen on a regular basis. It was as if the match incident was an announcement of things to come. More such experiences took place. I was not willing to admit to myself that my house was haunted, but in a very short time I changed my mind.

One night I was awakened by the sound of noise coming from the living room. I got out of bed and in the darkness, I fumbled and made my way to the living room. I was quite awake when I looked in the direction of the fireplace. There I saw the image of a woman kneeling at the fireplace opening. She turned her attention to me and then stood up. She was a small woman who was dressed in a long brown dress. Standing, she faced me and slowly began to fade until she was gone. That's when the emotion of fear really gripped me. I turned on every light in the house!

Weeks passed after this last incident before another strange occurrence took place. One morning, at about 11 a.m., I was walking from the bedroom to the living room. Suddenly an orange-yellow light came flying right past my left side. It appeared to come from the bedroom I had just left. It was a dull light; the color was like the light that a low-wattage yellow bulb would cast. It moved right by me, and as I followed it with my eyes, it moved quickly down the hallway to the living room where it disappeared! Of course, I had no explanation for this. My son, who was watching cartoons in the living room, also witnessed the light and screamed. I ran to my son and comforted him. Not wishing to alarm him any further, I reassured him that it was nothing to be concerned about. My own thoughts were, however, quite different.

After this last incident, we both began to see more examples of ghostly lights. Once, as my son and I were seated at the kitchen table having dinner, we both saw what I can only describe as a dancing spark appear on top of a family picture that was hung on the living room wall. The spark moved up and down around the framed picture, then leaped to the coffee table. It then flew up into the air and made two large tracing circles about the room before it disappeared. We were amazed at the spectacular light show and unable to find a cause for such a display.

Another afternoon, I was entertaining some neighbors I

had invited for lunch. We were all seated around the kitchen table talking. A neighbor named Cecilia asked me if I was aware of the strange lights in my house. She informed me that glowing lights were seen on several occasions by some of the neighbors. At the time that these lights were witnessed in the house, it was unoccupied.

Cecilia described the lights as "darting from room to room." Soon a rumor got around town that the house was haunted. Cecilia also told me about the original builders of the house, and the tragic history of the woman who had once lived here with her family.

One cold winter morning, the woman was placing wood into the fireplace and apparently got too close to the fire; her dress was ignited. Instead of immediately wrapping herself in a blanket or other covering to smother the flames, she ran screaming throughout the house. This action only fueled the flames to burn hotter and faster. Eventually, hearing the screams, her husband caught up with her and put out the fire. Although he did the best he could, it was obvious that his help had come too late. The woman suffered a lot of serious burns on her body and face. She was taken to a hospital in Phoenix, many miles away. He had to locate a car for transportation and then make the long drive to Phoenix, which at that time took most of the day. Due to the woman's loss of skin and severe shock, she died a few days after her arrival at the hospital.

After hearing the story of the burned woman, I decided to keep my own experiences with the ghost woman a secret. I did not want to draw any more attention to my house. This new information provided the explanation I needed to clear up unanswered questions. It must have been a very painful and drawn out death for that woman. I can't begin to imagine what it would have been like to experience such a horror. Luckily, my son was not present to hear the neighbor's story.

My response to the neighbors was only to say, "Well, I

haven't experienced anything like that at all since I've been here. Perhaps the lights everyone saw were caused by some kids playing with flashlights."

The only thing I felt I could do to get rid of any future hauntings would be to pray and seek the help of our local priest. The priest offered to bless the house, and nothing unusual happened during the blessing, just the usual holy water, prayers, and incense. After the house blessing I purchased a small picture of Saint Joan de Arc. I believe that due to the fact that this particular saint was put to death by fire, she might help in my situation.

I placed the picture of the saint on top of the fireplace mantle, and next to it a glass of water, which to me symbolizes the power to put out fires, along with any negative spiritual forces. I'm glad to report that after all these years, my son and I have not been visited by any more ghosts or lights. I hope everything stays that way from now on.

Winslow

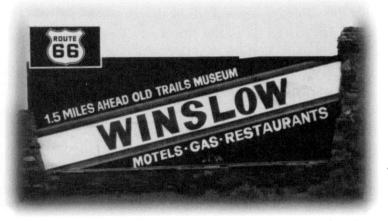

Winslow, which became a division point for the Santa Fe Railway, lies along Interstate 40 on the western border of Navajo County in the high plateau country of northeastern Arizona.

The community, at an elevation of 4,850 feet, lies in the Little Colorado River Valley, the river that skirts the city's eastern edge, 58 miles east of Flagstaff. Famed Route 66 was the major East–West route through Winslow before Interstate 40 replaced it.

The first settler, in 1880, was reputed to have been a hotel man who lived in, and did business from, a tent. Two years later, in January 1882, a U.S. Post Office was established. Incorporated in 1900, the town was said to have been named after Edward Winslow, a railroad company president. However, Tom Winslow, a prospector and early resident, claimed the settlement was named after him.

Winslow has a diversified economy—transportation, tourism, manufacturing, trade and retail business are important factors. The Santa Fe Railway and the Arizona Department of Corrections are the major employers with 500 employees each. Trade is the second largest employer, partly due to tourism brought in by traffic on Interstate 40 and Arizona 87, which connects Winslow to Phoenix. Arizona 87 continues north into the Navajo and Hopi Indian reservations.

My interview with Georgiana was conducted in the kitchen of the home of Georgiana's daughter, Doreen. As Georgiana and I readied ourselves for the interview, Doreen was busy at the other end of the table feeding her granddaughter an afternoon meal. I could not help but notice that Georgiana is a short woman, perhaps around 5'3". My attention was also drawn to her strong liking for silver and turquoise jewelry. Georgiana wore two bracelets on her left wrist, three rings on her right hand, and four rings on her left. She apparently also enjoyed the habit of smoking cigarettes, as throughout the interview no sooner had she finished smoking one, another was quickly lit with the remaining ember of the last.

Georgiana wasted no time in telling her story of what happened to her and her family while living in the town of Winslow. Here is her story.

GEORGIANA CHAMBERS'S STORY

I don't mind telling you that I am 64 years old. When the ghost began to appear to me and my family, I must have been about 12 or 13. My family moved to Arizona when I was just a baby. We settled in Winslow from the New Mexico town of Gallup. We never thought about witches or ghosts or any other weird things like that. We pretty much thought such rumors and talk was all "bunk." About the only people who mentioned ghosts were the Navajos that lived north of town.

Next to our home and property stood another home, which was owned by a husband and wife, James and Billie Mae Wakeman. This couple lived by themselves, as they did not have any children of their own. They had to be in their late 60s because they both had grey hair, and Mr. Wakeman walked with a

"Mother would dream of having such a comfortable home."

cane. They had a beautiful old house. The garden was always filled with gorgeous zinnias and huge sunflowers, which Billie Mae was so proud of. My brother and I were always hanging around the garden trying to capture the butterflies that were attracted to the brightly colored flowers. Mrs. Wakeman didn't care how long we spent at her house; I think she and Mr. Wakeman enjoyed having us children around.

Several times the Wakemans invited our family over to dinner. My mother was always impressed by how spotless they kept their home. Naturally, not having to pick up after children was the main reason. Since our family rented the house we lived in, it was always a dream of ours to actually own our own house. My mother dreamed about having such a comfortable home as the Wakemans.

Another dream my mother had was to have such beautiful hair as Mrs. Wakeman's. Mrs. Wakeman's hair was naturally curly, and she always wore it loose. Once I overheard a conversation that my mother and she had about hair care. Mrs. Wakeman informed my mother, "You know, the best thing for hair is rainwater. I have a metal rain barrel right outside the back door where I catch the rain off the roof and use it to rinse my hair. It's wonderful. I also like to add just a small amount of vinegar with the last rinse." Being a young teenager, I was fascinated. Although I never tried it myself, it sure did sound like a wonderful beauty tip at the time.

One March afternoon on Palm Sunday the following year, my family and I returned from church service. The year was 1921. I was in my room about to remove my church clothes when there was a knock at our front door. It was Mr. Wakeman. I remember he was very upset and in an anxious voice said to my parents, "Please, you have to come and help me. Billie Mae fell, and I can't wake her." We all rushed to their house and there on the kitchen floor we found Mrs. Wakeman. My mother and I began to cry. I was so scared. I had never seen anyone in such a condition before.

"The garden was always filled with gorgeous zinnias and huge sunflowers, which Billie Mae was so proud of."

The doctor was immediately called and after he had examined

Mrs. Wakeman, he sadly informed Mr. Wakeman that Mrs. Wakeman had suffered a heart attack and had died. It was such a terrible surprise to us all. Mr. Wakeman was devastated. They had spent so many years together, and now it was all over. He never fully recovered from his wife's death. As the months went by we noticed that he became weaker, and eventually he decided to move to the southern city of Phoenix. His younger sister lived in Phoenix with her own family and she decided that he would be better cared for living with them.

One day Mr. Wakeman invited my mother and father to his home and asked them if they would be interested in purchasing his house. My parents were surprised, but wasted no time in responding. Soon we moved from our rented home and into the Wakeman's. We now had a home of our own with a garden of flowers for my very own! Understand that we were all very sad to have gotten a house through such a sad turn of events, but the opportunity was given to us, and we were happy.

As the months passed, I recall a cold November night when I was asked by my father to go outside to the woodpile at the rear of the house. It was a cold night, and the fire in the wood stove needed to be fueled. I bundled up, and, with an old blanket to place the wood in, I went outside. I laid the blanket on the ground and began to stack the wood in a neat pile within the center.

Suddenly, I heard my name being called. I stopped my work and looked around. I didn't see anyone. Thinking it was my mother, I walked back into the house and asked who had called me. My mother said, "You're hearing things, Georgiana. Hurry up, now, I need that wood or else we're all going to freeze." Back to the wood pile I returned. I knew my name had been called out. I was sure of it.

I began to stack the wood on the blanket as before. Then I heard, "Georgiana, what are you doing, my dear?" I immediately stopped what I was doing, looked up, and saw Mrs. Wakeman!

I was so scared and wanted to run, but her ghost was

standing in front of the path that led to the house. I began to shake so much that I guess her ghost could sense my fright. Her ghost smiled a big, warm and loving smile. Although it was a dark night, I could clearly see her beautiful gray hair. Then, once again I heard her say in a whispering voice, "Dear, I'm alright. James is also going to be fine." My body stopped shaking, and it was then that I became aware of the tears that were falling from my eyes. As Mrs. Wakeman's ghost slowly disappeared, deep within me I felt a feeling of both sadness and happiness.

I returned to the house, and as I entered the living room, my mother came running to my side asking, "What happened, baby? What's wrong?" I was unable to control myself. I hugged my mother and cried out, "I saw her, Mother. Mrs. Wakeman appeared to me!" After a few minutes of consoling from both my parents, I explained to them what I had seen.

Although it was difficult for my mother and father to accept my story, they could not brush away the effect it obviously had on me. We all agreed not to mention to anyone what I had seen. Two days later, we received a letter from Mr. Wakeman's sister. She wrote that Mr. Wakeman had physically taken a turn for the worse and died in his sleep. My family was surprised by the news, but I was more than surprised. The reassuring words Mrs. Wakeman's ghost had spoken to me two nights before about her beloved husband, "James is going to be fine," now made sense to me. Her spirit had trusted me enough to give me the news about his death.

It was not long after the visit of Mrs. Wakeman's ghost that night that strange things started to happen in our house. Even my father was a witness to this.

At around 11 p.m. one night, we were all asleep in bed when we were awakened by the sound of noise in the kitchen. The noise was the sound that dishes make hitting against each other. Immediately, I thought that someone had broken into our home and was robbing us. I watched from the safety of my bedroom door as my father cautiously entered the kitchen. He was just a few feet away from the doorway when he suddenly let out a yell; "Get out of our house. You're dead. Please go. Leave now!" My father had seen the same ghost of Mrs. Wakeman that I had seen just a few nights before in our backyard. Although I did not personally see the ghost this time, my father's nervous reaction told the whole story. My father never explained to my brother and me what he had seen that frightened him so much that night. However, I did speak to my mother when my father was not around, and she told me what father witnessed.

It was just as I had thought. Standing in the kitchen that night was the ghost of Mrs. Wakeman. Father became a believer in ghosts that night and has since chosen not to discuss any such topic relating to the supernatural.

In the years following the last ghostly visit from Mrs. Wakeman, we have not seen or heard any more ghosts. My parents eventually sold the house to a couple from California who lived in it for a while, until it became too much to maintain and repair. One day it was torn down, and the land it stood on was left vacant for many years. I understand from the folks in the neighborhood that no improvements have been made to the property. One of these days, when I'm able to, I'd like to return to that old property and plant a couple of sunflower seeds in the ground. It would be nice to see flowers growing in Bille Mae's garden once again. I think she would be happy if I did that.

Yuma

Yuma is in the far southwest corner of Arizona, just below where the Colorado and Gila Rivers converge. Since prehistoric times, Yuma has been the best site for crossing the Colorado River. Yuma was named after the Yuman tribe, so called because of their habit of setting fires along the river (*humo* meaning smoke in Spanish). Fort Yuman was built during the gold rush to establish an Anglo presence in the area and to ensure a southern route into California.

First established in 1854 as Colorado City, the town became Arizona City and finally Yuma. Incorporated under the name Arizona City in 1871, it was reincorporated as Yuma in 1873 and now serves as the Yuma County seat. At an elevation of 138 feet, Yuma remains a crossroad for air and land transportation, although steamboats no longer carry supplies to mining communities and forts "up river."

Agriculture plays a dominant role in Yuma County's economy. Tourism, composed mainly of cross-country travelers and winter visitors, creates an estimated gross revenue of $368.8 million.

THE YUMA COUNTY COURTHOUSE

Built during 1928 according to the design of San Diego architects Ralph Swearingen and G. A. Hanssen, the third Yuma County Courthouse is a good local example of the Second Renaissance Revival style. The building was erected at a cost of more than $100,000 to replace a similar facility on the same site destroyed by fire on August 18, 1927. As the seat of Yuma County since 1928, the Courthouse has acquired additional significance as a symbol of government and as a distinctive landmark within the community.

THE HISTORY OF ADOLPH TEICHMAN

Within the apparent safety of stone and concrete walls of the courthouse are employees who have their own, very different story of a ghost whom they identify as being that of a former bailiff, Adolph Teichman. Mr. Teichman worked and lived in a loft above the second floor of the courthouse. He died on Christmas morning, 1949, at 82 years of age. In life, Mr. Teichman measured 5' 7", was hunched over, and was known to walk with a peculiar shuffling gate. His demeanor was quiet and friendly. City clerks who worked—and still work—the evening hours have witnessed an elderly, hunched man who walks the hallways in a shuffling manner. Could this be the loyal employee of the courthouse who now refuses to leave his former home?

Mr. Teichman is buried in Yuma at the northeast corner of Desert Lawn Memorial Park, next to his brother. There is no headstone to mark the resting place for either brother. Perhaps,

Mr. Teichman would now very much welcome a small token of appreciation from the citizens of Yuma. A small headstone per- haps? After all—death or no death—he still is very devoted to serving as caretaker of the courthouse. Just ask anyone who has worked during the late night hours on the second and third floors. He's around all right, still keeping a watchful eye on "his" courthouse.

My interview with Cecil took place in the maintenance office, located in the basement of the courthouse. During the inter- view, Cecil nervously chuckled and wrung his hands as he related his experiences. He was quite aware of the skepticism people might have towards his story, and the perplexed attitude of those who have never experienced a ghost for themselves. Undaunted by this, he presented a straightforward and focused account of what he believes to be behind the unusual activity that begins in the court- house when night falls.

CECIL J. ROACH'S STORY

As the maintenance foreman, I have been working at the courthouse for five years. Prior to working at the courthouse, I don't recall any stories of ghosts or hauntings being told to me. However, once employed and well into my job, certain individuals did feel comfort- able enough with my personality to open up and tell me about their own stories and expe- riences. Of course, I thought that behind these stories was another purpose. I thought people just wanted to have fun with me and get a good laugh.

Some of the secretaries have told me about their own ex- periences of seeing the ghost of an old man dressed in a suit. Some of them have refused to work in the evening hours be- cause of their experiences with the ghost. They say that the ghost resembles the photos of the dead caretaker, Adolph Teichman, who walks the halls. Doors will open and slam on their own. Also I've heard talk of file cards flying across the room while the secretaries are busy at their computers. They also hear footsteps and sometimes will even be touched on the shoulders. These things don't always happen just during the night hours. In the basement, during the day, workers have heard sounds of laughter coming from empty rooms.

Assistants who work with me have told me about seeing the same old man who walks down the hall and then gradually disappears. One assistant came to me one early morning yelling, "Cecil, Cecil, there's a bum loose in the courthouse!" He explained that as he looked through one of the glass windows built into an office door, he saw an old man moving about the room. The assistant attempted to open the door and confront the old guy, but it was locked. He described the man as being about 80 years old and wearing an old, worn suit. Another assistant told me about an old man who walked right past him, brushing against him in the hallway. When the worker turned to see where the old man was headed, he simply was no longer there. He had disappeared into thin air!

There also was an instance when one of the office service bells had, we thought, been stolen. It was missing for more than a year, then recently workers began to hear the sound of the ringing bell coming from the office. Maintenance workers informed me that they'd heard a ringing bell coming from that same office at 6 am. Of course, we looked and didn't see a bell, but just a few hours later, a secretary came to me holding the missing bell! She said that she had found it in the office and had no idea how it had reappeared after being missing for so long. What was strange to me was why that darn bell was ringing on its own in an empty office at 6 a.m.! It wasn't until I had my own first experience with the ghost that I began to slowly understand that I was working in a haunted building.

My shift always began at 3 a.m. I was given the responsibility of carrying the master key of the courthouse, and with that responsibility, I had to be sure to lock the doors behind me. Once in the courthouse I turned on the lights. I was always the only person in the building.

One night, 10 months into my job, I began to hear noises and footsteps of someone walking up and down the second floor hallway and slamming doors. I was on the first floor, and I recall going right up the stairs to see who was making all the noise. I looked all around and called out, "Is anyone here?" There was no response and no one in sight. This happened off and on for a few nights, then the noises stopped.

About a year later, at 4 a.m., I was once again alone in the building. I was buffing the hallway with a buffing machine, and over the soft humming sound of the machine, I began to hear the sound of someone whistling. I stopped the machine and listened to the fading whistle sound as it disappeared down the hall. I started up the machine once more. Again, the whistling began. I turned off the machine and walked up the hallway opening each office door and looking inside to see if I could catch anyone. The place was empty. Because I didn't see anyone in the flesh, I somehow got the courage to return to finishing up my job. I returned to buffing the floor. The whistling started up again, only this time it was right behind me! Yeah, I was concerned, maybe even a little scared.

After that odd experience, I had others. Sometimes when I'm working, I like to have my radio playing in the hallway to keep me company. The music also helps to keep me active in the early hours. As soon as I would leave the hallway or room, it would shut off on its own! I thought perhaps there was an electrical problem with the outlet or even with the radio itself. As I returned to where I placed the radio, I noticed that the radio's electrical cord was lying on the floor, disconnected from the wall! Now, this might sound strange, and it might appear to be a problem with a certain

"As I began to walk past the door, it opened wide and forcefully!"

wall outlet, but even stranger was that this happened on every floor and wall outlet I plugged the radio into.

My choice of music was not the only thing that the ghost did not like. My coffeemaker was also unplugged. Sometimes I brought my coffeemaker with me and plugged it into a wall where I was working. When I returned to see if the coffee was done brewing, I discovered that the cord had been pulled from the wall, just like my radio. One time I returned to find the extension cord I had connected to the coffeemaker was also disconnected and was wrapped around a trash can with one end inside the can! Now, how can anyone explain that?

Soon I began to notice these strange things happening more frequently in the month of December. Even stranger, the activity would intensify as the days got closer to Christmas. One year, at about 5 a.m., as I was getting out of the elevator on the second floor, a voice loudly called out my name, "Cecil, Cecil!" Of course there was no one in the elevator with me, but I turned around anyway just to be sure. I saw no one. Now, that really scared me and gave me goose bumps.

Just last year, two days before Christmas, I had an assistant helping me in the building. I was on the second floor where the courtrooms are located. Suddenly, I saw one of the doors to a courtroom open. Since the courtrooms are to be locked securely due to strict security procedures, I immediately investigated.

I entered the courtroom, turned on the lights and looked around cautiously. I saw no one. I then locked the door behind me and walked down the hall. I came upon the door that lead up to the top floor where Adolph Teichman used to live. As I began to walk past the door, it opened wide! When this happened, I moved so fast, I don't even remember how I reached the first floor!

Not long after, I was with another assistant when we had a joint experience so frightening that even to this day, I can't get it out of my mind. Again, it took place in the morning hours. We were both seated in

"I saw a large black ball floating down the stairs!"

my office talking, when suddenly we heard noise coming from the hallway. The noise was of someone hitting and spinning the lid on a trash can. Thinking that this unusual noise was caused by a security guard who had entered the building, we waited for him to come to my office and pay us a visit. After a few seconds had passed, I got up out of my chair and checked the hallways and doors. The doors were locked, and I assumed that we were the only ones in the building.

We disregarded this latest strange experience and soon got back to work. My assistant climbed the stairs to the third floor, and I remained on the first floor. Everything was going as usual until I heard a noise and then saw something coming down the stairs. You might think I'm crazy, but as I looked to the stairs, I saw a large black ball floating down the stairs, with a smaller black ball following behind! The larger ball was the size of a basketball. The smaller ball also followed the larger ball by about four feet. They were traveling quickly, as quickly as someone running down the stairs might move. As the balls reached the landing, they disappeared. I can't explain the thoughts and feelings that went through me. I was shaking and covered in goose bumps. I can't say any more about that night. It was a very frightening thing to witness.

Throughout the years, I have heard and seen lots of things in this building. There is definitely something here. I know there is. Because I still work in the courthouse, I would rather not see any more ghosts, or hear whistling and the ringing of bells, or other sounds again! I mean it! I want the ghost to know that I want to be left alone.

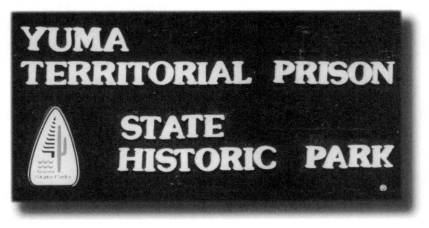

YUMA TERRITORIAL PRISON

On July 1, 1876, the first seven inmates entered the Territorial Prison at Yuma and were locked into the new cells they had built themselves.

A total of 3,069 prisoners, including 29 women, lived within these walls during the prison's 33 years of operation. Their crimes ranged from murder to polygamy, with grand larceny being the most common. A majority served only portions of their sentences due to the ease with which paroles and pardons were obtained. 111 persons died while serving their sentences, most from tuberculosis, which was common throughout the territory. Of the many prisoners who attempted to escape, 26 were successful, but only two were from within the prison confines. No executions took place at the prison because capital punishment was administered by the county government.

Despite an infamous reputation, written evidence indicates that the prison was humanely administered and was a model institution for its time. The only punishments were the dark cell for inmates who broke prison regulations and the ball and chain for those who tried to escape. Prisoners had free time when they handcrafted many items to be sold at public bazaars held at the prison on Sundays after church services. Prisoners also had regular medical attention and access to a good hospital.

Schooling was available for convicts, and many learned to read and write in prison. The prison housed one of the first "public" libraries in the territory, and visitor's fees for tours of the institution were used to purchase books. One of the early electrical generating plants in the West furnished power for the lights and ran a ventilation system in the cell block.

By 1907, the prison was severely overcrowded, and there was no room on Prison Hill for expansion. The convicts constructed a new facility in Florence, Arizona. The last prisoner left Yuma on September 15, 1909.

The Yuma Union High School occupied the buildings from 1910 to 1914. Empty cells provided free lodging for hobos riding the freights in the 1920s and later sheltered many homeless families during the Depression. Townspeople considered the complex a source for free building material. This, plus fires, weathering, and railroad construction, destroyed the prison walls and all buildings except the cells, main gate and guard tower, but today these provide a glimpse of convict life a century ago.

LINDA D. OFFENEY'S STORY

My present position at the prison is as Park Ranger 2. My duties require me to be the curator, tour guide, and front desk clerk. I've worked at the prison as a ranger for over 14 years and have lived in Yuma for a total of 18 years.

Before working here, I never gave the matter of ghosts much thought. Now, my thoughts have changed, because I can not explain the strange things that we all have witnessed.

One night, alone in the facility, I began my usual evening security check of the prison grounds. Walking outside the museum, I made my way toward an area of the prison known as the dark cell. Years ago, when the prison was in use, this particular cell was used as punishment for those prisoners who were not following the rules. It was solitary confinement. The dark cell to this very day is not a very pleasant area to visit. As the name implies, it is dark and very eerie.

As I continued with my security check, I walked over to the dark cell and proceeded to check the iron gate located at its entrance. Suddenly, I felt the presence of someone gazing at me from within the cell. I was overcome with a feeling of fear. I had made the same check many times before, but this time something was different. This time, the hair on the back of my neck stood on end. I didn't actually see anything, but I sure did feel the horrible gaze of something staring back at me. I quickly made sure that the gate was locked and hurried away from that area. Returning to the comfort and safety of the museum, I thought about what had transpired and just could not shake the feeling of those eyes staring at me.

As a point of information, in our files is a picture that was taken in the late 1930s of a woman standing by the cell block area where the dark cell is located. The woman is not the ghost, but in the background behind her is the figure of a ghostly man. He appears to be outfitted in a World War I uniform. The soldier is standing in the archway to the left of the opening to the dark cell. The rangers who have seen the picture think that this room—which is now walled up—is where the insane prisoners were kept until they were transferred to an outside asylum. The woman is apparently unaware of the ghost standing just a few feet away behind her.

Another strange occurrence at the prison is when visitors report to me that they have been pinched while in the dark cell. I began to notice a pattern that these guests all shared; they all wore clothing where the dominant color was red. It made no difference if they were in the company of others or by themselves. They got pinched! Keep in mind that these were visitors who were unrelated and came to my desk at different times of the year. I can't explain it.

Another day, I took a tour of children into the dark cell. I gathered them all around and told them the history of the cell and, not wanting to frighten them, I kept the information as much as possible on a pleasant level. Well, in the middle of the tour I had a child who was wearing red clothing state to me and the group that someone had just pinched her! I tactfully ended my talk and escorted the children out the door.

Three years ago we had a visiting staff writer from *Arizona Highways* magazine pay us a visit. She wanted to do a story about the prison and got the strange idea of spending two days and nights in the dark cell—alone. She wished to "experience" the isolation that a prisoner might have had in years gone by. She even asked to be chained by her foot to the cell, as a prisoner would have been. We provided her with a jug of water and loaf of white bread and placed a heavy blanket over the entrance to the cell to keep out any sunlight. We also provided her with a makeshift toilet, which brought a smile to her face.

In memory of the inmates, who lost their lives while serving their sentences, at the Arizona territorial prison at Yuma. Of the 3,069 convicts sentenced to Yuma Prison, 111 died there. Disease, accidents, murder, suicide, and escape attempts were the causes of their demise. The remains of 104 unfortunate souls are interred in this cemetery.

She had anticipated to remain in the dark cell much longer than she did, but she soon discovered that she was not welcome. As she described it, she began to sense the presence of someone else in the cell with her. She began to feel pinching or prickling sensations all over her body. We soon heard her alerted calls to us to get her out of the cell quickly, which we did.

Before I end my story, I do want to tell you about a unusual character that dwells inside the museum, whom we all refer to as "Johnny." There were evenings when I was at the cash register totaling up the day's money. A strange thing happened. As I had the register drawer open, suddenly, the coins jumped out! It was as if an invisible finger was flicking the coins out of the drawer compartments.

There were also other times when I was standing over the

opened cash drawer with a hand full of coins. The coins suddenly jumped out of my hand and into the drawer! Now, is that strange or what! Other staff workers have also seen this happen. "Johnny" does not seem to be interested in paper money, just coins. We don't know who this playful ghost is, or why he is so interested in money. He still performs his antics every now and then with us.

There are other unusual things that have happened here. The local people in town have reported to us that they have seen lights from oil lanterns moving about the prison in the evening hours when it is closed. These lights have always been seen in the cell block area of the prison. We have visitors and staff who have reported incidences of hearing voices of men in low conversation. These are usually heard in the museum area.

My own personal attitude about ghosts in the prison is that they will not hurt me. I just know they won't. More of a concern to me is encountering a rattlesnake or skunk that might have decided to venture into the facility. We have had such unwelcome visitors in the past. However, if I were to actually see the ghost of one of the prisoners, I would like to sit down and ask him a question or two about his experiences. I know it would scare me to death, but I would still be interested.

JESSE M. TORRES'S STORY

Currently, I am the assistant park manager and have been employed at the prison for over 16 years. I was born and raised in Yuma, and because the prison is so familiar, I didn't really think much about it as a historic site. Little did I know that one day I would be responsible for its well-being.

Before working at the prison, I had heard stories in town about the place being haunted. I'm basically a skeptic, so I didn't

Outside Cell 14

pay these stories any mind. I used to think that if I ever felt or heard anything which might be paranormal, it had to be my imagination. That's what I *used* to think.

My first experience with ghosts at the prison took place when I was about eight years old. I was brought to the prison during a school field trip. As the school group was led through the grounds by our teacher, we passed an area of the prison named the "New Yard." The group was walking ahead of me as I lingered in front of cell number 7. Something drew me to this cell, and as I looked inside, I saw a man dressed in a striped prisoner uniform standing inside the closed iron door. At the time, I felt uneasy and quickly ran to keep up with my classmates.

The museum staff has had visitors tell us that they have also seen a prisoner in that very same cell, dressed in prison-striped clothes!

Eight years after I began working at the prison, I had an experience I have never forgotten. The current storage room in the museum used to be used as an office by the staff. One day, as I was in the museum cleaning the glass cases that hold artifacts of daily prison life, I heard voices coming from the office. Knowing I was alone in the building, I stood still and listened. The voices were the soft whispers of men in conversation. I clearly heard one or two words that I recognized, but I was unable to make a complete sentence out of them. Thinking that some unauthorized person was in the building, I quietly walked to the office door, took hold of the door knob, and opened the door. Once I turned on the light, I saw that the room was completely empty; the voices I had just heard a few seconds ago were now gone.

Another early morning, alone in the museum, I clearly heard a voice demand, "Jesse, did you get it?" Startled by such a request, I turned around to face the person. I saw no one. I felt the hair on my neck stand right up!

Another experience in the prison took place in the old cell block, directly outside cell number 14. One winter day, as I was walking down the cell bock area, I walked past cell number 14. A movement in the cell caught my eye, and as I looked through the spaces of the iron door, I saw a ghostly figure moving about inside! Other staff members have also see this figure, and have heard its footsteps as it moves about the cell. Visitors who know nothing about the history of cell number 14 have approached us to say that they have heard a noise and have felt the "heavy presence" of someone in the cell.

From old prison records, I discovered some information about a prisoner named John Ryan. As listed on the prison records, his was a "crime against nature." In early prison history, "crime against nature" was a label given to prisoners who had committed rape or other such acts of sexual deviation. The records also showed that Mr. Ryan did not get along well with the other prisoners and was placed alone in cell number 14! While in the cell, he committed suicide by hanging himself with a rope made from his blankets.

Description of Convict
Name: John Ryan
Number: 1660
Crime: Crime against nature
Sentence: 5 yrs. from 9/28/1900

photo courtesy of Yuma Territorial Prison

John Ryan

County: Coconino
Nativity: Iowa
Legitimate Occupation:
   Miner/Cooking
Age: 31
Habits: Intemperate
Tobacco: Yes
Opium: No
Religion: Catholic
Size of Head: 7⅛
Size of Foot: 8
Color of Eyes: Gray
Color of Hair: Light Brown
Married: Yes
Children: 3
Can Read: Yes
Can Write: Yes
Where Educated: Iowa
When and How Discharged:
   May 6, 1903 Committed suicide
   by hanging in cell 11:30 a.m.

Prison Record

NOV. 10, 1900: Solitary, 3 days for fighting
MAR. 12, 1901: Solitary, 11 days for striking a fellow convict
MAY 27, 1902: Solitary, 4 days for Insubordination
SUPT.'S REPORT, MAR. 31, 1901: Report about his being
   temporarily demented.

   In another area of the prison is a cell named the dark cell.
The staff has had several visitors narrate to us that when in the
dark cell, an unseen entity—or ghost—pinches them. Some visitors feel such a negative presence that they have refused to enter
the room during our ranger-guided tours. Once, a man stated
that while visiting the dark cell, he saw moving and flashing

lights. He said he was not about to stay in there another moment and quickly left.

When it was in use, the dark cell was a form of punishment to any prisoner who fought, was caught stealing, or tried to riot. Within the dark cell was a large iron cage with two iron rings at opposite corners. First, the prisoner was stripped down to his underwear. Next, the prisoner's legs were chained—one leg to each iron ring. His only food was plain bread and water. The prison records do not mention any prisoner ever dying while in the dark cell, but the records do state that at least two prisoners did leave the dark cell, only to be immediately transferred to an insane asylum in Phoenix.

I think that there are spirits trapped in the walls of the prison. But I find it strange that the prison cemetery lacks any ghostly activity. One would think that of all places on the grounds to be haunted, it would have to be the cemetery. I don't go in for such stuff as ghosts or hauntings, but what we have seen here does cause me to wonder.

HOPI
(Hopituh)

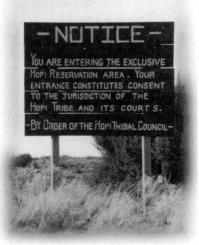

The Hopi reservation lies within the larger Navajo reservation in the northeast quadrant of Arizona. The nearest town of Tuba City is located to the west while the largest city of Flagstaff is located to the southwest. The Hopi area itself is quite isolated by many miles of desert and canyons. Highway 264 provides the major access to and from the reservation. When mentioning the Hopi or Hopituh nation, it is difficult not to focus on such essential elements as farming and gardening. Existing and thriving in a desert environment is testament to the adaptive ability of these unique and deeply spiritual people. Hopi can trace their physical ancestral birth to their homeland as being approximately 1200 and earlier. Archaeologically, garden terraces at Third Mesa or Bacavi prove this. Farming methods used in times past are still in use to this day. Examples are the ingenious use of gardens located on mesa walls, which are irrigated terraces that are water fed by the villages located above. Another method is "dry farming." This technique involves the planting of seed within arroyos (washes) and valleys located on the lower plateaus where seasonal rain produces the moisture necessary for their germination and growth.

The Hopi cosmology is composed of four worlds, or "ways of life." At the present time, the Hopi believe that they are in the fourth way. As they moved from the third way to the forth way, they and other people were offered corn by the creator, or Ma'saw. Aside from the Hopi, all the other people eagerly and boldly

Hopi village

took the largest of the corn that was offered. The Hopi in turn were left with the shortest and smallest blue corn. The Hopi immediately knew that this was symbolic of their life to come as it too would be short and difficult. Thus, their response was to manifest the virtues of cooperation, humility and respect among themselves and others. They also knew that the earth was a wonderful and giving, living spirit and its healthiness would depend on the Hopi people as its caretakers. Today the Hopi live in four separate and autonomous mesas or villages, and within each village are sub-communities. First Mesa includes Waalpi (Walpi), Hanoki (Hano or Tewa), and Sitsomovi (Sichomovi). Second Mesa includes: Songoopavi (Shongopavi), Musungnuvi (Mishongnovi) and Supawlavi (Shipaulovi). Third Mesa includes Hoatvela (Hotevilla),Paaqavi (Bacavi), Munqapi (Moencopi), Kiqotsmovi (Kykotsmovi), and Orayvi (Oraibi).

DONALD FIRST CRY'S STORY

Me and my girlfriend Becky are both Hopi. I've spent most of my life on the reservation, except when I left to work for eight years in San Diego, California. My older brother and I were offered well-paying jobs as roofers in new home construction. Becky has worked at the reservation school cafeteria for just a couple of months, and we plan to get married next year. My experience with a ghost took place two years ago. Up to that time I had never had any kind of spooky stuff happen to me. I know that a lot of ghostly things do take place in the hills and mesas that surround our tribal lands, but I never really paid much attention to the stories. Anyway, two years ago Becky and I spent a summer weekend in the gambling town of Laughlin, Nevada. We never thought this short get-a-way was going to be anything but a fun time. We've driven together to Laughlin many times before without ever having encountered a ghost. So this first weird experience shook us up for a long time afterwards.

When ever we've driven to Laughlin, our normal routine is to arrive at a hotel, check into a room, then hit the "one arm bandits" downstairs. We've both done this since we were in our early twenties. Sometimes we win big, and some-

times we lose, but we have a good time nonetheless. This time, we arrived at the hotel on a Friday evening at around 7 p.m. We checked into a room on the 14th floor with a view of the Colorado River below. We emptied our suitcases of clothes, which we hung on hangers in the closet. Then we decided to watch a little television before heading to the lobby downstairs for a bite to eat. As at other times, we both knew we would spend most of the night gambling, so we were in no hurry.

As we were lying on the bed watching a comedy show, I felt an uneasy feeling come over me, a feeling of depression that I had never experienced before. I thought that maybe I was getting the flu or had gotten food poisoning from lunch. I felt a sort of a weird "thickness" come over me. I know it sounds strange, but I felt like a cold mud had covered me. I couldn't make sense of why I was suddenly feeling so bad. At one point, I looked away from the television and out the open window. Without being conscious of it, I began to think crazy thoughts of darkness covering me like a cloud. I began to shake like a leaf. My heart was throbbing and I was filled with a sense of dying. Becky must have noticed something was up, because I felt her hand touch my shoulder and say, "Donald, Donald what's the matter?" I answered, "Nothing, I'm just not feeling too good. Maybe I'm getting a cold or the flu." I told Becky that I needed to close my eyes and rest, but she looked at me funny and said, "You're drenched in perspiration, Donald, just look at you." I told her that I would be all right, but I needed to relax for a few minutes. Becky sat back on the bed, but kept an eye on me.

I turned my attention back to the television, and soon I began to feel better. Then that feeling of disaster came slowly over me once again, and I automatically began to glance out the window as before. I thought I was having an anxiety attack, because my hands began to shake and a feeling of fear began to take control of me. A friend of mine once had an anxiety attack when we were at a restaurant, so I am aware of the symptoms. I yelled to Becky, "Look at me; something is happening to me!" Becky came to my side and said, " Donald, what is it, what's going on?" After a few seconds, I decided to get up off the bed and walk to the bathroom, and splash water on my face. Becky followed, and looking at me through my reflection in the mirror, said, "Donald, should we take you to a doctor? You might be having a heart attack." I answered, "No, no let's just go get something to eat." As quickly as this thing came over me, it left. I soon regained my composure and told Becky that I was feeling much better. Whatever it was that had come over me was now gone. We decided to leave the room, go down to the lobby and get some dinner.

I began to feel much better and even got lucky when I won $800.00 playing the $1.00 slots! At about 2 a.m. we decided to call it a night, and took the elevator to our room on the 14th floor. Getting ready for bed, I brushed my teeth, then closed the drapes and got into bed. We both quickly fell asleep, but my sleep did not last for long. I was awakened a few hours later when Becky grabbed my arm and shook me hard. "Donald, Donald, wake up, wake up, there's some guy in the room!" Becky said that she had awakened with the strong feeling of someone's eyes staring at her. When she opened her own eyes she saw the figure of a young man standing next to the bathroom door. Out of fear she grabbed my arm and woke me from my sleep. I watched as Becky pointed me to look by the bathroom. At first, I didn't see anyone and then I heard a loud "thud!" It sounded like someone had fallen to the floor. I leaped out of bed and cautiously turned on the lights. As I looked around the room, I noticed there was nothing out of place. As much as I could tell, we were alone in the room. I carefully walked to the closed bathroom door, reached for the knob, and opened it. I reached inside and felt for the light switch, then turned it on. There was no trace of anyone. Although we could easily explain away the figure of the guy Becky had seen as being a bad dream, we could not explain the falling thud sound we had both heard. Throughout the night, we would hear the thud sound again and again. Being too tired to stay up any longer and discuss it further, we returned to bed and fell asleep. The next morning Becky told me she was unable to sleep and was awake most of the night.

After breakfast we walked to the parking lot, got into our car and drove to the local mall to do some shopping. We entered a dress shop where Becky began a conversation with another customer who worked in the same hotel where we were staying. She introduced herself to us and said she was a prep-cook there. The woman was a Paiute Indian from California and she and Becky hit it off right away. I excused myself, and decided to wait outside the store on a bench, while Becky had her conversation. When Becky caught up with me, she told me that the woman had given her some strange information about the hotel where we were staying. Apparently, three days before, there was a guy who had unknowingly killed himself on the 14th floor of the hotel. He was a drug addict who mixed a batch of heroin in the bathroom of his hotel room and died of an overdose. While doing her job, the maid found the body the next morning. The Paiute woman had informed Becky of this because Becky mentioned to her that we were staying on the 14th floor. Although the woman was unaware of the dead man's room number, she told Becky it was a room that had a window that faced the river below. The cook also had Becky promise that she would not tell anyone at the hotel about what she had said, for fear that she would lose her job.

Well, this new information sure did give us a new perspective. Becky became very nervous and told me she did not want to worry or scare me, but that the figure she had seen in our room the night before appeared to her once again that night. She told me that she did not get much sleep because the ghost made a sound that caused her to look in the direction of the bathroom. Once again, she spotted the ghost standing against the wall, in a leaning position. His eyes were dark black, and opened wide, and even though his mouth moved to make words, no sound came out. Then the ghost suddenly disappeared. Becky said she closed her eyes and convinced herself that what she had seen was something her imagination had made up, but she spent the night drifting in and out of sleep. With this new information, Becky and I returned to our hotel and demanded a room change. Since that weekend, we've not had another experience with the supernatural. And I have not had another anxiety attack or anything like one.

HUALAPAI

In times past, beginning around 600, the Hualapai were a tribe who were primarily hunter-gatherers. But where water was available, the Hualapai cultivated gardens of corn, squash and beans. Today there are just under 2,000 Hualapai who live at the tribal headquarters in Peach Springs, Arizona, 50 miles east of Kingman on Historic Route 66. The total reservation encompasses 108 miles of the Colorado River and a segment of the Grand Canyon. The topography of the reservation varies from rolling grassland and shear, rugged canyons to pine forest. Elevations range from 1,500 feet at the Colorado River's banks to over 7,300 feet at Aubrey Cliffs. The Hualapai nation has managed to maintain their culture, language and well-deserved pride. The future looks positive for the Hualapai, especially since they currently have one of the highest number of students who are enrolled in college of any reservation in the state.

ROBERT RED SKY'S STORY

One winter in the month of January, when I was seventeen, my brother and father, along with my father's two good buddies, went on a deer-hunting trip in the Hualapai valley. This was a hunting trip that none of us will ever forget. Even now a strange feeling comes over me when I think back to what we all witnessed years ago, on what started out to be just an ordinary outing. That winter day I experienced an example of the power of spirits that come forth from the land the Hualapais call home.

Two weeks before, my father had spoken to three Indian fellas in town. These guys mentioned to him about the big deer bucks they had seen browsing and running within a deep canyon. To offer further proof, they asked my father to walk with them out to the road where their pick-up truck was parked. The men proudly pulled off a large plastic tarp which was covering the bucks they had killed. He told me those guys had some of the most beautiful bucks he had ever seen. He asked the three guys for detailed directions regarding the location of their successful hunting. As they gave him directions, he wrote down every road, turn and curve. In our Indian way, we don't hold back information about such hunting areas. It's traditionally right that we share such information among our people, and it's something that goes back a long way with the Hualapai.

My father arrived home and told my brother and I about the deer. Soon we had planned a hunting trip. My father was convinced he too could shoot a deer or two just like those guys in town had. He got on the phone and invited two good friends of his. The date was set.

We knew the weather would be cold so we packed a good supply of food and warm clothes. My father enjoys eating hot chile so my mom made him about two dozen beef burritos with some very hot red chile, all rolled up in foil. These he planned to heat up on the camp fire. We loaded the pick-up with three days supply of food and water, the burritos and our hunting

"We soon came to the main turn-off from the highway."

gear, then off we drove to meet up with my father's two friends.

We started out in the early morning, and although it was a very cold winter morning, there was no snow on the ground. The weather was perfect. We soon came to the main turn-off from the highway. It was a dirt road which was not too rough for the first five miles but then got very rough as we made another turn on to another road. The sun was already up in the east as we started our way up over a hill. We stopped at the top of the hill and took a short coffee break. As we stood standing around the two trucks in the empty landscape drinking our hot coffee, we suddenly heard a strange sound come from the west. It was like the sound of a hundred hoofbeats, the sound of many horses going at a full gallop. It came from nowhere; it just sort of started up and lasted for a few seconds, then it ended. We expected to see a herd of horses come up onto the hill, but there was nothing visible, not even a dust cloud. None of us could explain what it was. We nervously joked about it being a flying jet, but the sky was, as far as we could see, clear of any aircraft. Not saying another word, we finished our coffee, got back into the trucks and continued on our way.

The time now was eight-thirty in the morning and I could tell that the trucks were not going to be able to continue any further on the very rocky road we were driving on. We decided to stop and make camp in the middle of a distant, small grove of juniper trees. The wind was still and the air was cold and crisp

*"We followed an old coyote trail that went down the
eastern side of a ridge."*

as we opened our tents and arranged them around a rock fire
ring that my brother formed. After making camp we decided to
eat some food, and then head out with our rifles towards the
hills in the direction we were told the deer would be. We followed an old coyote trail that went down the eastern side of a
ridge. We were careful not to talk loudly, or make loud sounds
with our footsteps. Deer are very alert and can be easily spooked.
We noticed that the area was littered with deer droppings. A
good sign! The area was sparsely spotted with medium to tall
junipers, and in the distant narrow valleys were a few groves of
cottonwoods and oaks. My father knew that deer like to browse
in these areas, so we were constantly trying to pick out any
movement in the distance. Suddenly, just as earlier before, the
weird sound of hoofbeats started up again. We all stood still and
waited. Then, just as before, the sound came toward us and soon
disappeared. This time we were not so quick to dismiss the

sound as being a jet plane. We softly spoke among ourselves, but said nothing about it being an omen of bad medicine. We knew it would not be a good thing to talk about it any further, because to do so would bring us a bad hunt.

We again picked up the hike and continued towards the valley below. The time was now one in the afternoon, three hours since we left our camp site. As we entered the valley and the grove of tall trees, we were startled as a porcupine came out from behind an old stump and gave us all a fright. It was difficult to keep from laughing loudly. We all felt a sense of relief at our little friend's sudden appearance. As we exited the other side of the grove of trees, my father, who was now walking ahead of us, spotted some deer on the side of the hill. He stopped his walk and lowered his left hand, exposing the palm, which was a signal for us all to immediately stop. We stood still and viewed the deer, quietly scanning the large herd before us. There were ten does and three really beautiful bucks. What a sight! This was what we had all dreamed of. We spoke in soft voices, communicating to each other how best to get a shot at the bucks. Then, without warning, something scared the deer. They must have seen something big or dangerous because they bolted and went running. They couldn't possibly have seen or caught our scent among the trees. We automatically got down on our bellies and watched as the deer darted just a few yards away from us. We froze like statues, trying to camouflage into the surrounding brush and trees. Just as it appeared that the deer were going to reach us, they darted in another direction and disappeared behind a small ridge.

We were speechless, and wondered about the sudden change in the deer. We thought there must have been a hungry mountain lion or something very scary that had attempted to attack them. We rose to our feet and looked toward the area where the deer had been grazing and did not see anything unusual at all, not a mountain lion nor even a bird. Nothing.

Things were now becoming too strange for us to dismiss all these experiences. Something other than coincidence was at work here. My father spoke first and said, "I think we should perhaps offer a prayer for guidance and asked for protection from whatever is tracking us in these hills." My father's two older friends agreed and in our native language we all bowed our heads and prayed.

After praying, we decided to continue tracking the deer and headed in the direction of their escape. It didn't take long before we found ourselves in another canyon walking between tall stone walls.

A small stream of water bubbled out from a large sandy area which formed a shallow pool of water. All around the outer edges of this pool were green, mossy plants and deer tracks. We knew we had found a deer water hole. The only problem was that we were a long hike away from our supplies and shelter. We knew that it would be better to head back to camp and start out earlier the next morning. We climbed up and over a large pile of boulders, then hiked along the canyon wall for a short distance, then headed up and out of the canyon. We made it over the boulders with no trouble, but when we began to hike along the canyon wall, my brother called to my father to look at something on the walls. There on the walls were some ancient petroglyphs, stone pictures which were carved on the canyon walls centuries ago by pre-historic native people. These carvings were not the usual ones which we were accustomed to seeing on

"There on the walls were some ancient petrglyphs."

other walls in other canyons. These were not pictures of sun, bird, stars and lightning symbols. These were pictures of people without heads, or with the heads and arms of animals. There were pictures of owls and figures with opened mouths. My father and his friends spoke out loud, "These pictures tell that this canyon area is full of supernatural forces. The pictures of headless people mean that bad witches and animal spirits were working together to make bad medicine here many years ago." We all agreed that to get out of this canyon as soon as possible, would be the best thing to do.

We hurried our hike and soon reached the top of the canyon. We reached our camp just after dark. We got dinner going on the fire and after eating our fill, drank a few cups of coffee. Not once did we mention the weird sounds, the deer's reaction or the petroglyphs we had experienced that day. In these times it is best to not talk about such things. To do so, we believe, would call to us the dark forces. We decided at around eight that evening to call it a day and get into our sleeping bags. After placing some more wood in the fire we all stretched out, close to the fire ring. We were very tired from all the hiking of the day, and were eager to get enough rest for the next day's activities. Very soon after zipping up into our bags, we fell into a deep sleep. I must have been the last one to nod off because I remember hearing everyone's snoring before falling asleep. The next thing I remember is being suddenly awakened by a loud snapping sound coming from one of the burning logs in the fire. I opened my eyes and stared at the black, moonless sky above. I remember thinking to myself, what a beautiful sky it was, as I viewed all the stars filling the dark spaces from one vast direction to the other. Then I turned to face some movement which caught my attention in the brush a short distance from our camp. I saw what looked like a naked person crouching down on his legs staring at me! I thought that I must be imagining this because of how tired I was. I closed my eyes and rubbed them with my cold fingers. I again turned my attention to the figure in the distance and sure enough, it was still there, just staring at me. I began to get scared, thinking it might be someone who was going to rob us. I knew that my rifle was just a few feet away from me, but I would need to react quickly in order to do any good.

As I observed this person, I realized that he was the size of a child. I watched as he made a quick motion and stood straight up. That did it for me. I threw off the sleeping bag and yelled for everyone to get up as I went for the rifle. I yelled," Hey, there's a guy over here." Everyone reacted quickly by jumping out of their sleeping bags. I told them about the person I had seen in the bushes. My father listened to me and then said,"I had been seeing that guy for some time before you woke us. There are other spirits with him as well. I've been seeing two more of them moving from juniper bush to juniper bush." This got my brother a bit scared. He spoke: "Well what are we going to do. Will they hurt us, do they want us to leave this place?" My father's friend responded: "I think we should pack up and leave this place. These are not good spirits. We saw the pictures on the rocks; those are not good pictures. Those are pictures of witches and people who work with bad spirits. I really think we should leave this place tonight." We threw more wood on the fire and we got it burning brightly. We decided to take my father's friend's advice and leave the canyon that night. As we packed up our gear, I again noticed the shadows of people, or spirits, running from bush to bush. I let the rest of the men know what I had just seen. My father decided to sing a prayer and the rest of us joined in. My father's friend then ended the prayer by announcing, in the direction of the spirits, that the creator was watching over our well-being and that they should leave us alone. Suddenly, we heard the low sound of laughter and hoofbeats leave our camp. This is when I knew our power of prayer helped us chase away what ever was watching us.

We all got in our trucks and drove home that night. We

did not speak again about our experience until the next morning. During breakfast we told our mother about our experience. She said that during the day and night we were gone, an owl had been making hooting sounds in the tree in our front yard. This was very unusual and she knew that this was an omen that something bad was happening to us. She herself began to pray for us to return safely home. Aside from this experience I have had a couple more that have taken place, but I don't think I'd like to talk anymore about this.

SAN CARLOS APACHE

The San Carlos Apache Indian Reservation is located east of Phoenix in southeastern Arizona and was established by Executive Order on November 9, 1871. The total land mass of the reservation is just under 1,900,00 acres. The reservation was reduced in size a total of five times for the benefit of copper and silver miners and eager Mormons whose demand for water surrounding the Gila Valley reduced it further. It is the seventh largest U.S. reservation, with over 7,100 people. Within the reservation borders are forested alpine meadows and wooded mountains, as well as desert plains. Anthropologists speculate that the Apache nation entered this region around 1450. The San Carlos Apache call themselves "t'iis ebah nnee" or "grey cottonwood people" and their language is closely related to the Di-neh' (Navajo). The San Carlos Apache now consider themselves to be a unified people, even though their history shows they were originally several separate bands of the same Native nation.

After his surrender in 1873, the great Apache chief Cochise, along with his followers was forcibly taken by the U.S. military to San Carlos. Soon after, the famous medicine man Geronimo and his followers fled the oppression of the San Carlos Reservation.

Presently, the reservation fights the continuous battle of arduous unemployment among its people, with the hope of further developing industry and tourism. Encouragingly, tourism is taking hold as a source of income and employment. The tribe is directly promoting its lakes and forests, focusing on campers and sportspeople. The cattle-ranching industry and the mining of Peridot, a semiprecious stone found within the reservation, is also a source of employment. The largest nearby town of Globe provides needed medical and shopping facilities.

HENRY TALL HORSE'S STORY

My mother died when I was two years old, and since that time, I've lived in San Carlos with my father. My experience was with two spirits. Everyone seems to think that ghosts only appear during the night, but in my case, I saw them during the day. These spirits didn't harm me, but I still got pretty scared. My experience was a strange and powerful one that I know will stay with me for a long time.

One spring morning, when I was nineteen years old, a close friend and I decided to walk over to the nearby San Carlos river and fish for catfish. Before heading out, we found two metal beer can openers. We used two stones to pound them flat, and made them into spear points. We sharpened the metal points, grinding them against a large flat boulder. Then we wrapped each of these points with wire to the ends of long thin, but strong, poles. It was a primitive but effective tool in spearing fish. My friend and I went fishing like this many times before, so we were eager to catch a lot of fish. It was about 10 a.m. when we got to the river. We followed the river bed until we found a spot with a few trees to shade us from the sun, and a pool of water that we hoped had some fish. We each sat on the sand at opposite sides of the pool. Because the pool of water was a short distance from the main river, the water was still. In this still water, it was easy to spot the movement of swimming fish. We fished for a few hours, and caught five fish. We decided to head home and fry the fish for lunch. Most Apache I know don't like to eat fish because of our traditional beliefs, but that is changing. My friend and I enjoy eating fish. After our catfish lunch, my friend went home to his house and I took a nap.

Around 6 p.m. I decided to walk back to the river, only this time I just wanted to walk and not fish. I followed the path back to the pool of water where my friend and I had been earlier. As I got closer, in the distance I heard a very strange sound. The sound was a humming or buzzing noise that I couldn't identify. I decided to investigate by following the sounds up the river bed ahead of me. The sun was starting to go down in the west, but there was still plenty of light. As I got closer, the noise seemed to change to something like the flapping wings of a large flock of birds. I decided to slow my pace in order not to surprise whatever might be making the noise. I walked as carefully as I could through the trees and spiny weeds. I had a feeling that animals might be nearby, so when I thought I was close enough, I stopped and got behind a large tree branch to hide myself. Flies were buzzing around my head, but I didn't want to make any noise by swatting them. I got down on my stomach and lay flat on the sand, so I wouldn't be seen. In the distance, not far from me, I could see two large shadow-like figures. They were about 70 yards away from me and I was unable to make out what they were. At first I thought they were two large dogs. They were about the same size as german shepherds. I strained my eyes to see the figures. Suddenly they changed into a shape that looked like a human figures! They were definitely not dogs, and I knew they

were definitely not human either! As I said before, there was
plenty of sunlight, so darkness was not a problem. Also, something like cloth, or maybe even animal skins, hung loose over
their bodies. I couldn't tell what this stuff was. The figures had
arms and legs, hands and feet, and their faces were covered with
this cloth like stuff. This covering made it impossible to a make
out their faces. I saw them bent over on their hands and feet,
walking just like a four legged animal.

While I was watching all this take place, coming from the
direction of the figures was the flapping wing noise that I had
heard earlier. There were no birds anywhere and no wind blowing either! But I could hear the noise of what sounded to me
like a tremendous flock of birds' wings flapping! These mysterious figures stood up, bowed down, turned around, and slowly
moved away from each other. Several times they got down on
all fours, and for many minutes, turned in complete circles. It
seemed like they were dancing. Something inside told me that
these "things" were not normal, but in fact "spirits." I was
scared. I tried my best to keep very still, but I was shaking all
over. After a few minutes, the spirits changed their steps and
began to move from side to side. I know this might sound crazy,
but the figures changed from animal to human to animal and
back again. I couldn't believe what I was seeing! Suddenly, they
did something that scared me even more: they stood upright on
their feet, and leaped towards each other. I'm telling you, this
really surprised me. I didn't expect them to do this, or to be so
fast. I felt that if I moved, even a finger, they would discover me.
Who knows what they would have done to me. Because they
were moving all around the riverbed so much, I was afraid they
would eventually spot me. I decided to keep lying flat on my
stomach, hoping to camouflage myself as much as possible. If
they spotted me, I was ready to run for it. I kept quiet and
watched them repeat their strange dance over and over again. A

few times one of them would jump about ten feet into the air. It was terrifying and, at the same time, fascinating to watch.

I stayed hidden behind the branch for a few more minutes, until I felt a bug sting my leg. I felt it crawl into my pant leg and sting me on the ankle. It must have been a wasp because it hurt like heck! I didn't want to make a sudden move, but knew I needed to get rid of it. I slowly sat up and stretched my arm over to scratch my leg. Through it all, I didn't take my focus off the spirits. Luckily, they didn't notice me. But when I turned my head, I hit it against a branch that was a few inches above me. The sound of the moving branch gave me away! I saw the spirits freeze and immediately they turned their heads in my direction! I saw them crouch down and instantly disappear into thin air! That was all I needed. I stood up and ran for my life, breaking branches as I ran through the bushes. Several times I lost my balance and fell to the ground. Each time I got up and ran back down the river retracing my steps, stumbling many more times before arriving at the road which led back home. It's difficult for me to describe how scared I was. I was shaking all over.

When I got home, my father saw me covered in sweat and dirt and asked me where I had been. I excitedly told him the story of what I had seen. He looked at me with a strange gaze that I had never seen before and shook his head. He said, "Those were not things you should have been watching. You should not have been sneaking up on those spirits. They need to be left alone when they dance. You must not ever sneak up on spirits again." He also told me: "The spirits come down from the mountains from time to time." They have been doing this since Apaches first came to this area. The spirits live in the mountains and canyons. They follow the water because there is power in water. The river is like a big vein and water is the blood of life for spiritual beings. You need to go back there to where you saw the spirits, and leave them an offering." I told my father that I would do as he said, but as of this day, I have not gone back to that spot.

I don't want to see any more spirits. Knowing that the spirits did not wish to cause me any harm has changed my view of spiritual things, but I'm still not wanting to meet any more of them. I was raised with the stories of spirits that lived in the nearby mountains around our reservation, and was told of witches and ghosts that took many animal forms. Years ago it took my own personal experience with the dancing spirits to prove to me that these were not just stories. I know these spirits are real because I have seen them.

White Mountain Apache
(Nde, Indeh or Tinneh)

The White Mountain Apache have the notable history of being the direct descendants of the original Apache tribes who settled the area many centuries ago. The ancestral homeland of the White Mountain Apache Nation is located in the east central region of Arizona. The Apache are now a nation comprised of several independent bands throughout the Southwest.

The reservation encompasses 1.6 million acres. It was established by Executive Order on November 9, 1891. Strongly traditional in culture and spirituality, the nation currently has over 12,000 members. Historically, they were hunters and raiders who did some farming, but in many cases carried out raids on neighboring agricultural-based villages for food that they were unable to obtain by hunting. The Apache consider the mountains that surround their lands to be holy and the source of their spirituality. The Spaniards, Anglos and Mexicans were unsuccessful in their numerous attempts to subdue these true guerrilla warriors. As with almost everything ever written about the Apache, it is important for the reader to question the source of the written word, due in large part to a negatively-skewed view regarding the Apache being linked to vast amounts of atrocities. In fact, this cautious approach should be taken when reading most anything printed about Native People—period.

Today a wide range of accommodations that include dining, shopping and gaming at the Hon-Dah Casino are available on the reservation.

CATHERINE TWO BEAR'S STORY

In 1992, I was attending the University of Arizona in Phoenix. I was in my senior year and majoring in biology. During the summer of that same year, five seniors (including myself), four graduate students and a professor were conducting field work at Theodore Roosevelt Lake. The Lake is located in the Tonto National forest, about a two-hour drive northeast of Phoenix. Our two-month study and research focused on native amphibians of the lake, specifically bullfrogs. Throughout the years, this particular species of frog had begun to change the ecology of Arizona's lake and streams. Although the bullfrogs had increased in populations, other smaller native population of frogs were showing the beginning signs of extinction. Bullfrogs have a voracious appetite and will consume anything smaller than themselves, including snakes, other frogs, lizards and mice. Our focus of study was to specifically record data, and ultimately discover a link to the bullfrog population explosion.

Although I enjoyed the research field work, it was wet, muddy, smelly and I had to wade in waist-deep cold water. In order to catch the frogs, I had to dress in water-tight rubber overalls. Also part of my uniform was a net laundry bag which

I tied to my belt, a pith helmet with a flashlight strapped on top, and of course a fish net attached to a four foot pole. I and my colleagues would get in the water at about eight in the evening and begin our "hunt," which would last until around ten or so at night. We initiated a process of surprise by which we would catch these fast and alert bullfrogs by slowly wading towards a floating mass of leaves or plants. Using the light strapped to my helmet, I would scan the area until I spotted the bright tell-tale sign of a bullfrog's reflecting eyes. Once spotted, I would make my way towards the frog, careful not to make any ripples and, using my fishing net, quickly catch it and place it inside the net bag tied to my belt. This system, although primitive, would bring in about ten to twenty frogs a night per student. Each pair of students had a section of lake in which to capture the frogs. After finishing our work for the night, we would drive back to the lab and place the frogs in a large stock-water tank for study the next day. Our evening captures took place three nights a week. Due to the many frogs in the area, we had enough specimens and paperwork to keep us very busy.

So what does capturing bullfrogs have to do with ghosts? Well, one evening during a night of bullfrog catching, something very, very strange happened to me. Another girl and I went off for the evening to do the night's frog-gathering. We went into the water at about eight in the evening. The frogs were making their croaking sounds as usual, and we got right to work. But at about nine o'clock, I began to feel sick. My stomach was turning. I figured it was something I had eaten earlier at dinner. I decided to end the evenings hunt and get back to my warm bed. I informed my partner that I would be taking the truck, and for her to catch a return ride to the lab with the others. "No problem," she said. So off I drove. The road was dark. I had to drive slowly due to javalinas (wild desert pigs) and other small animals that were out and about. It was summer, so to get fresh air, I had both the windows in the truck lowered. Suddenly, I felt something come in through the passenger side window! Something hit the right side of my body and gave me a terrible scare! I quickly put on the brakes and nervously turned on the interior truck light. Then I saw it—a small owl! Apparently the owl had flown across my path on the road, and mistakenly entered the truck through the open window. Well, there it was, on the floor of the truck flapping its wings with its beak wide open. I can look back now and say, that confused bird gave me a good scare! I opened my drivers' side door and scrambled outside. I walked over to the passenger side door and opened it, to allow the owl a way out. But when I opened the door the owl was gone! Where had it gone? I carefully looked under and behind the truck seat, but there was no owl. If it had exited the truck on its own, I would have heard it, or even seen it because the light was still on inside the truck. This was definitely a strange thing that had just occurred. The owl in my truck simply disappeared! Knowing something about animal behavior, I knew that this was not usual. Also, being an Apache gave me a cultural knowledge about such things. Traditional Apache people do not consider owls to be positive animals to be associated with. I knew this owl was not a good omen. Owls to Apaches are messengers of bad news, and even death. My parents have told me that some medicine people who do evil use the owl's spirit in their witchcraft.

I quickly got back into the truck, rolled up both windows and drove at a fast speed to the cabin. I admit that at the time, I was scared being all by myself. When I entered the cabin, I went straight to the bathroom and showered. I still had the stomach ache, but now I was more concerned about my recent owl incident. After making sure that all the doors in the cabin were locked, and the outside light was on, I got into bed and waited for the return of the others. After about twenty minutes, no one had returned, and I began to get worried. I got out of bed and looked out the window, and saw nothing but darkness. I thought it best to try and sleep, even though my stomach was a ball of nerves. As soon as I got back into bed, I heard the sound of footsteps in the front room. I knew there was no way someone could have entered the cabin without opening the locked door and making a sound. Something bad was definitely going on, and I was scared! As I gazed from my bed at the open doorway that led into the bedroom, the footsteps stopped. Then there was silence for a few seconds. Soon I heard the voice of what sounded like a small child say in my Apache language, "Can I go see mama, I want to see Mama, can I go see mama?" I couldn't stop trembling. The words were very clear, and because they were spoken in Apache, that made them even more terrifying to me. I had had enough of this, so I jumped out of the bed and, in the darkness, scrambled for the light switch on the wall. Nervously, I tripped over my own shoes, fell to the floor hitting my left shoulder, and smashed my big toe against the dresser. I was in pain. I figured my toe was broken. I managed to crawl across the floor, then find the wall with the light switch, turn it on, and crawl to the bathroom.

No sooner had I entered the bathroom, I heard the sound of my fellow students' trucks returning to the lab. I was an emotional mess. I decided it would be best not to tell anyone about what had happened to me. After all, what could they say or offer me? One thing that I did need was to get some medical help for my toe. It was already swelling up when my roommate came in the door. I told her that I had fallen, and that was all. I was driven that night to the student university clinic in Phoenix, where an x-ray was taken, and I was given the good news that the toe was not broken. Still it hurt quite a lot and was very bruised. Unable to do any more night wading for frogs in cold lake water, my research ended. I spent the remainder of the summer at home. Once I arrived home, I told my parents all about the experience with the owl, and the child's ghostly voice. They told me to pray and to never again be out alone in that area. My parents could not offer an explanation regarding the owl that came into my truck, or the ghostly voice of the child. All I was told was that sometimes these "things" are forces that foretell a future event. As of this date, I have not had anything happen to me that I can connect to that summer night in 1992. But, that does not mean I won't. I'm hoping not to ever experience anything like that again. I'm not the type of person that goes looking for ghosts and things. Ghosts scare me.

YAQUI NATION
(Yoeme)

Culturally, the Yaqui or Yoeme nation is descended from the ancient Uto-Azteca, or Mexica people of Old Mexico. In the year 1533, the Spanish made contact with the Yaqui, and ultimately Christianity was introduced, which profoundly altered the Yaqui way of life. Interestingly, the Yaqui embraced Catholicism and the new Spanish system of government, but always kept an independent stance in this union. The Yaqui religious life of today is a result of this merger of ceremonies and cultural beliefs. San Ignacio's Day Fiesta, Easter and Christmas are the most important ceremonies of the year for the modern Yaqui. The Yaqui have a history of being fiercely independent, and resisted Spanish colonialism until 1610, when a treaty was signed between the two. Originally they occupied eight villages in the state of Sonora, Mexico. Due to Mexican political changes, they migrated north to Arizona.

The Yaqui nation was not recognized as an "historic tribe" by the U.S. Bureau of Indian Affairs until 1994. Their battle for such recognition was long and difficult. Considered political refugees because of their migration from Mexico, they were denied the services afforded to other American Indian nations, and thus not recognized as a independent nation and reservation. Presently the population numbers just over 9,000. In Arizona, the Pascua Yaqui Indian Reservation was annexed into the city of Tucson in 1952. The tribal land, 222 acres, was established in 1964 by an Act of Congress and is surrounded by a desert landscape of scenic vistas, drives and trails. The San Ignacio fiesta is observed at Old Pascua, a village located in Tucson that marks the annual fulfillment of the village's obligation to its patron saint, St. Ignatius of Loyola. The Yaqui also currently operate the successful Casino of the Sun. There is another group of Yaqui that reside close to Tempe and Phoenix in the town of Guadalupe. It is from this town that the following story was obtained.

BENJAMIN RED OWL'S STORY

My one and only experience with a ghost took place when I was twenty- six years old, in the summer of 1991. Up to that point, I can't remember ever having had any type of a paranormal experience. Of course there have been times when I've overheard friends and family discuss such things as ghosts and haunted areas, but I've never given the subject much attention. All this changed for me during one summer night in Montana. I had completed four years of graduate work in Art History at the University of Colorado, and with a master's degree under my arm, I made plans to give myself a break from all my hours of study. I thought that rewarding myself with a trip to Canada would be a nice change. Also, I knew that once I entered the job market, it would be a long time before I would have the opportunity to travel for quite some time. In fact, I already had two job offers waiting for me once I returned home. I was in no hurry to return to an office, so I was very eager to begin my trip.

My reason for driving all the way up to Canada was to visit Jerry, a Cree Indian friend, whom I met while attending school.

Jerry lived in the province of Alberta, and was a real joker of a guy. Among us Indian students, Jerry was known for his wacky sense of humor. I couldn't wait to get on the road. I packed my small Toyota with all the necessary camping gear—tent and snacks—then got on the interstate heading north to Wyoming, Montana, and my ultimate destination, Canada. Along the way, I spent nights in public campgrounds which were located in state and national parks. Before leaving the northern-most portion of state of Wyoming, I spent six days in the town of Sheridan. Another friend from college, Tom, lived there. Tom is a Lakota Indian who graduated two years before me with a degree in Marketing Management. Tom told me about his friend Joseph who lived in the town of Billings, north of the Crow Indian Reservation. Tom gave Joseph a call and arranged for me to spend a couple of nights at Joseph's house. Joseph was known as a maker of award-winning horse saddles. Tom and I said our good-byes, and off I left to continue my journey north.

I took my time, stopping frequently to take pictures and observing the beautiful prairie landscape. Because of my many sight-seeing stops, I arrived at the Crow Reservation late in the evening. I turned off the highway and found a rest stop where I made camp for the night. In the morning I packed-up my things and drove to the nearest restaurant, got breakfast, then drove to the Little Bighorn Battlefield Monument to have a look. Given its history, and I being Native American, the battlefield was a unsettling place to visit. The Monument's Visitor Center was filled with historical paraphernalia. Being a history buff, I spent a good two hours reading the informational texts, and taking in all descriptions of the artifacts on display. Reading about the major battle that was fought and jointly won by the Sioux and Cheyenne against the invading General Custer was fascinating. I felt proud to be Native American, and at the same time, saddened knowing the present social state that most Indians are locked into. After a few hours, I got in my car and drove on the two-lane road which meandered through the battlefield itself. At one point, I decided to park and go for a hike over the rolling hills and small valleys of the battle site. As I said earlier, I had an uneasy feeling about the place. Standing on the actual ground where the battle was fought many years ago gave me an eerie feeling. I didn't at all feel frightened, just uneasy. After spending several hours hiking about the area, evening was approaching and it began to get dark. I decided to head back to my car, where I had a quick dinner of warm coke, an apple and cookies. Billings was about an hour or two away, so I got back on the highway, anticipating that I'd have a bed at Joseph's house. This plan, as it turned out, was not to be.

After just a few miles on the highway, I noticed that my car was strangely jerking. I knew something was going to give out. Sure enough, just after getting on the interstate, my car altogether stopped. I got out and pushed it to the side of the road. Because I had been told by a mechanic back in Denver that the car's fuel filter needed to be changed, I suspected this was the cause of the problem. I had the foresight to buy a new filter before I left on my trip. Because it was already too dark to get under the hood and replace it, I decided to tackle the problem the next morning. After all, it was not a very long, difficult job to change out the old filter for the new one. Maybe a total of 30 minutes, max. Not far up ahead, I noticed a flat area with tall trees. I decided to push my small car over to this area. I parked the car away from the highway traffic. It seemed like a safe camping site for the night. All the hiking earlier in the day had tired me out. I couldn't wait to get into my sleeping bag and fall asleep. I opened the car's trunk, took out the sleeping bag, and lay it on the ground, with the car creating a buffer between me and the highway. I soon fell asleep.

Sometime during the night, I was awakened by the touch of someone stroking my neck. Because the stroking feeling was not at all sudden or discomforting, at first I was not frightened. Then the thought hit me that someone, a stranger was touching me! I opened my eyes and, still lying in my sleeping bag, I turned around. I gazed in the direction which I imagined a person would be standing. At first I saw nothing in the darkness. Then I saw some movement to my left. My heart was beating hard and I was getting anxious. I turned to look to my left and I saw the image of a small Indian girl. She startled me, and I think I let out a little yell of surprise. I immediately knew this person was a spirit, because her image was vapor-like. She was the same luminous color as the moon, and I could see the trees right through her. I got scared and thought I was going to have a heart attack. I couldn't move. My body was trembling. I don't know why I couldn't find the strength to get up and run. It was if my body was locked with fear. The ghost stood about five feet away from me with a very sad look on her face. She was dressed in a yellow-colored dirty dress, and wore several necklaces made of big beads. She just stood there in front of me staring. I tried to speak, but my voice was weak and my throat was dry. One thing I do remember clearly was the strong scent of wet grass. It was a very earthy scent that I can remember to this day. It's difficult to explain, but I was able to smell and to "feel" the odor of mud, water and grass of a long time ago. It's weird, I know, but that's how I can explain it.

Soon, and with much effort, I managed to get out a yell. She then began to fade away, beginning at her feet and ending at her head. I yelled again, and soon it was all over. She was gone. Sweat was dripping down my face. My ghost encounter took place in what appeared to be all of about five minutes. I got out of the sleeping bag and jumped into the front seat of my car. I locked all the doors, turned on the radio, and after some nervously exhausting minutes pasted, I managed to fall asleep. In the early morning I was awakened when a large noisy semi-truck passed by on the highway. Inside the car, as I moved around, I felt something at the back of my neck. I reached my hand up to scratch, and was surprised when I felt a hardened substance which had attached itself to my hair. I pulled some of this off and looked at my hand. It was hardened mud! I pulled more of this hardened mud off of my neck and head, then I carefully opened the car door, got out and shook the remainder of the dirt from me. I didn't know what to think. Did I have a bad dream during the night, and roll on the ground? Or, did the apparition of the ghost woman rub this mud on me? I didn't care to think anymore about the mud. Frankly, I was eager to repair my car and get the heck out of there!

Now that there was plenty of morning sunlight, I replaced the fuel filter in my car, and after several false starts, got my car going again and hit the highway. Driving north on my way to Billings gave me a few hours to think about what I had experienced the night before. I couldn't believe that I had seen a real ghost just a few hours before. I had lots of questions, with no answers. But the most disturbing question of all was, why did she cover my neck with mud? Was she trying to heal me of an injury? I soon arrived at Joseph's house. Joseph was not home, so I asked his whereabouts at a neighbor's house. After introducing myself to the older woman, she informed me that her neighbor, Joseph Dances Straight, was dead. Apparently, two months prior, while visiting his sister in South Dakota, Joseph and two friends went hunting for deer. One of the shotguns accidently went off, and the blast hit Joseph at the base of his skull, killing him instantly. I was caught off guard by this information. The neighbor was not willing to give me anymore information. I could tell that she and Joseph were close friends. I left her house filled with a numbness. Eventually, I arrived at my friend Jerry's house in Canada. I told him about what I had experienced during my short trip, the ghost woman, and finding out about Joseph's death. Jerry got seriously quiet, then told me that I had been visited by an Indian spirit messenger in the form of a woman. Also, because earlier in the day I had immersed myself in a powerful area—The Little Bighorn Battle Ground—I had "opened myself up" to a spiritual visitor. He went on to say that the messenger had rubbed "medicine" on my neck which symbolized the manner of death which had taken Joseph.

After spending two weeks with Jerry, I returned to my home in Arizona. Never will I forget about my experience with the ghost in Montana. There are lots of things that us Indians need to be aware of. I know that modern society is a very powerful force, but we need to respect and honor our traditions from long ago. These are also very important, and necessary for our people.

Other Books
by Antonio R. Garcez

New Mexico Ghost Stories
Originally published as
The Adobe Angels New Mexico series
ISBN 0-9634029-9-4

American Indian Ghost Stories
of the Southwest
ISBN 0-9634029-7-8

Ghost Stories of California's
Gold Rush Country and
Yosemite National Park
ISBN 0-9634029-8-6

For more information on these or Antonio's future
books on the supernatural, please contact:
Red Rabbit Press
4129 N. Gold St.
Silver City, NM 88061

About the Author

Antonio R. Garcez graduated with a B. A. degree from California State University at Northridge, then attended Graduate school at the University of Wisconsin. Antonio resides, and continues to write from, his home in New Mexico.